FLYING TIGERS

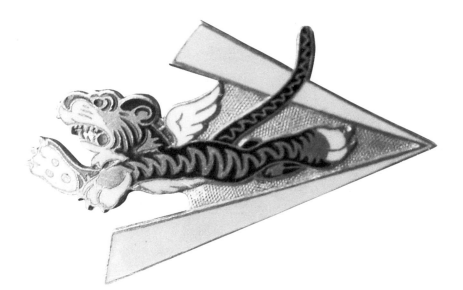

FLYING TIGERS

PAUL SZUSCIKIEWICZ

GALLERY BOOKS
An imprint of W.H. Smith Publishers Inc.
112 Madison Avenue
New York, New York 10016

Published by Gallery Books
A Division of W.H. Smith Publishers Inc.
112 Madison Avenue
New York, New York 10016

Produced by
Brompton Books Corp.
15 Sherwood Place
Greenwich, CT 06830

ISBN 0-8317-2672-5

Printed in Hong Kong

10 9 8 7 6 5 4 3 2 1

CONTENTS

PAGE 1: A Flying Tiger pin, as designed by the Walt Disney Studios.

PAGE 2, ABOVE: A leather breast patch worn by the American Volunteer Group.

PAGE 2, BELOW: One of the P-40s of the 3rd Pursuit Squadron.

LEFT: The jagged teeth and staring eye made famous around the world by the Flying Tigers.

FOR the majority of East Asians World War II broke out on 7 July 1937 when a battalion of the Japanese Kwantung Army clashed with the Chinese garrison of the town of Wanping, near Peking. This event was the culmination of over 40 years of tension between the two great Oriental nations and opened what both sides believed to be the final round of their fight to dominate the region. It also set in train a series of events that were to make legendary figures out of a former US Air Service aviator of weatherbeaten appearance and his selected band of American fighter pilots.

When the vain attempts of both China and Japan to keep out the modern world began to fail in the middle of the nineteenth century, the two countries chose very different approaches to coping with the Western powers. The Japanese recognized that

ing relationships and agreements on China that ate away at the country's national integrity and sovereignty. Japan's rulers considered the Celestial Empire to be well along the road to extinction, and clearly comprehended the possibility of gains from bullying their neighbor. When the Boxer Rebellion broke out in 1900, Japan openly sided with China's predators, joining the Westerners to suppress the movement and ravaging much of northern China.

Taking the side of the Boxers had been the last gamble of China's conservatives. The Chinese were reduced to the impotent status of hapless spectators during the next major conflict in East Asia, the Russo-Japanese War (1904-05), when Japan humiliated Imperial Russia in a battle for control of Manchuria, the national homeland of China's ruling Qing dynasty. Rebellion and

CHAPTER 1

WAR IN CHINA

their technological inferiority would prevent the waging of an effective resistance and embarked on a program of modernization. Their society was adapted to conform to modern ways, but traditional attitudes were maintained to preserve its character. The Chinese, however, chose to redouble their efforts to repel the modern world, and repeatedly went down to defeat. By 1895 even their Japanese cousins were able to crush them in battle and kick them out of Korea.

Japan's elite saw the world in Darwinian terms: a continuous struggle between predatory nations and social forces to alter or preserve an international pecking order. This vision compelled them to intervene in Chinese affairs. China in the late nineteenth century was subject to a similar process as the 'Scramble for Africa,' with the European colonial powers engaging in a kind of 'tussle for China.' Each was attempting to gain access to a prospective market of millions. To achieve this they imposed special trad-

revolution, this time directed against the empire and its Confucian bureaucracy, broke out in 1911 and the Qing dynasty abdicated the following year.

A battle for control of the Middle Kingdom between an assortment of regional warlords and visionary Nationalists began. This opportunity was not wasted by those Japanese who were bent on eliminating China permanently as an effective rival in Oriental power politics. They forced concessions from the new Chinese republic. Hoping to gain influence, they did nothing to discourage radical Chinese from pointing to Japan as a role model for their country's twentieth-century development. In the early 1920s the Japanese government was so confident in its position as the leading power of East Asia that pressures for more concessions from China were greatly relaxed. However, Japan's window of opportunity began to close with the triumph of Chiang Kai-shek's Nationalists in 1928.

LEFT: Japanese troops in northern China search civilians for contraband. The Japanese were cruel overlords in the lands they occupied, which stimulated the Chinese will to resist.

BELOW: Artillery bombards Chinese positions in Nanking, while infantry stand ready to advance. The Japanese attacked Chiang Kai-shek's capital in December 1938.

RIGHT: The Japanese promised 'harsh and relentless treatment to the defenders of Nanking,' and were as good as their word. The 'rape of Nanking' was a loathsome display of human cruelty.

BELOW RIGHT: Chiang Kai-shek and Madame Chiang with Claire Chennault.

Though the unity of the new China was fragile at best, and though the very backwardness of its economy promised only a long and hard journey toward modernization and international competitiveness, the merest glimmer on the horizon of a strong, modern and united China was enough to cause Japan alarm.

Japan's ruling classes – the army, the civil service and the business elite – were torn apart in a bloody internal struggle over China policy. Politicians and soldiers were assassinated, mutinous army officers attempted putsches, and a few, a very few, murderers and mutineers were tried and sentenced. By the middle of 1936 the supporters of a 'positive policy' toward China triumphed. To their eyes it was just in time. In December 1936 Chiang Kai-shek finally agreed to establish a united anti-Japanese front with the Chinese Communists, ending a bitter, if desultory, civil war that had been going on between them. For the first time since 1900, Japan faced an almost undivided Chinese regime that was determined to make no more concessions and no accommodations with the major powers, Western

or Oriental. It was inevitable that the resulting tension would lead to a fight. The matter of when was settled at Wanping's Marco Polo Bridge in July 1937. The Japanese Army was better organized and equipped than the Chinese, and by 1939, after two years of war, Japan controlled all of northern China, a good deal of central China, and most of the ports along the east and south coasts.

The United States had observed Far Eastern developments from 1900 to 1937 with an indifference that became increasingly nervous. China had for long been attracting American attention. A good many of the East Coast establishment's fortunes, especially those belonging to Bostonians, had been based on trade with China. It was also a popular destination for missionaries bringing the message of the Christian Gospel. American policy toward China was based on the so-called 'Open Door' principle – that all nations should have access to an independent China on equal terms. The tantalizing vision of the China market – in truth something of a phantasm, never amounting to more than three percent of total US trade – being lost forever to US commerce, and the reports of the terrible atrocities perpetrated by the Japanese, especially the notorious 'rape of Nanking' from December 1938 through February 1939, transformed gradually the US attitude of strict neutrality into one of supportive sympathy for the Chinese.

The first US efforts to aid the Nationalists, hampered by an unwillingness on the part of the State Department to antagonize Japan, were limited to loans to help finance civil purchases and sales of commodities. But when the Japanese established a puppet republican regime in Nanking during the spring of 1940, even the State Department conceded that China was in danger of being 'lost.' The loan program was stepped up, and the money could now be spent on arms.

Chiang Kai-shek was especially keen to revitalize his air force, which had suffered very badly at the hands of its more modern Japanese counterpart. In October 1940, after taking advice from his financial consultants, he summoned his aviation adviser, Claire Lee Chennault, and suggested that the Chinese Air Force buy some American planes and get American pilots to fly them. Chiang Kai-shek asked Chennault if he would accompany a purchasing mission to the United States, and make some inquiries concerning the prospects of getting the pilots. Chennault agreed to go, and the creation of the American Volunteer Group (AVG) in China now became inevitable.

CLAIRE Lee Chennault was born on 6 September 1893 in Commerce, Texas. On his father's side he was a kinsman of Sam Houston, while his mother could proudly claim to be a relative of the Confederate hero Robert E. Lee. He was raised in the rural surroundings of Franklin parish, near the small town of Gilbert in northeastern Louisiana, a part of America's Deep South. Here his father owned a small cotton farm, run with a few black sharecroppers.

Chennault had his first taste of military discipline at the age of 16, when he enrolled at the Louisiana State University. In those days the students were called cadets, and their school was housed at the Pentagon Barracks in Baton Rouge. He was unable to finish his schooling, however, as monetary misfortune and a plague of boll weevils damaged his father's finances. Trying to

by this time, with World War I concluded, America's need for combat pilots was somewhat reduced. Peacetime soldiering did not initially appeal to Chennault and he was honorably discharged from the Air Service. Chennault soon changed his mind, however, and applied for a commission after seeing in a newspaper article that the Army Air Service was looking for pilots. By September 1920 Chennault was back in khaki. He was assigned to the 1st Pursuit Group, but was later transferred to the 12th Observation Group which patrolled the Texas-Mexico frontier.

During the 1920s, while China was the domain of rival warlords, and the United States did not let Prohibition prevent its indulgence in the Jazz Age, Chennault advanced up the Air Service promotion ladder. Between 1923 and 1926 he was in com-

CHAPTER 2

CHENNAULT'S TIGERS

decide what profession to take up, Chennault found that Louisiana was investing heavily to improve its then rudimentary educational system. Chennault went to college and became a schoolteacher, but the pay was not sufficient to meet his expenses. He had married in 1911, and with his wife had begun a family. He drifted from job to job over the next few years. He moved north and found himself working in a tire factory at Akron, Ohio, in April 1917, when war was declared by the US on Germany.

Chennault volunteered for the US Army and applied for flight training. He was rejected, but accepted for officer training, and on 27 October was commissioned a first lieutenant in the infantry reserve. He transferred to the Signal Corps, where he worked in an observation balloon section. His repeated applications for flight training were rejected, but his luck changed in October 1918. At last he was accepted into flight school, and graduated on 9 April 1919. But

mand of the 19th Pursuit Squadron which was stationed in Hawaii. After his tour of duty there, this now-experienced aviator served as an instructor at two training establishments. At the Air Corps Training Center in San Antonio, Texas, Chennault was involved in some of the first American experiments with paratroopers. As a result, he was approached by members of the Soviet Union's trade organization in the United States and asked if he would like to help the Red Army to organize a parachute unit of its own. The terms were attractive: a five-year contract at $1000 per month, plus expenses, together with the rank of colonel. However, Chennault declined, partly in fear that he might lose his American citizenship if he served in another country's armed forces.

His refusal also was due to his appointment to a course at the Air Corps Tactical School. Institutionalized organizations have strong prejudices, and the Air Corps upper

LEFT: The sight that gave heart to many a Chinese soldier during 1941-42: a P-40 of the Flying Tigers. Claire Chennault's scheme had finally come to fruition.

echelons were filled with men who had been to West Point or flown over the Western Front during the Great War. Chennault did not qualify for command on either count. The Tactical School might, however, be a route to further promotion and responsible command.

It did lead to his appointment to the school's staff as an instructor, and Chennault found himself in the midst of a debate that was to have profound consequences for the kind of doctrine that the Air Corps would adopt. On one side stood the advocates of bombardment; on the other the apostles of pursuit (fighter) aviation. Around the globe air services were engaged in attempts to get out from under the thumbs of the armies that had nurtured them through their early days in World War I. In Britain, the RAF had escaped, while on the other side of the world the Japanese did the opposite, leaving the army and navy to organize their own respective air services. The principle of the independent air force, the dream of all aviators, was invariably developed out of the vision of massed fleets of bombers which supposedly would be able to get through an enemy's aerial defenses and attack the vital centers of his economy. These would then be destroyed and the war won easily. Only an independent air arm made up of similar fleets could defend against this danger by providing a deterrent. There were aviators who thought the bombardment argument failed to appreciate the ability of fighters to defend a state against air attack. To their minds the war of the future would still have to be fought and won by an army's ground forces. An air force's duty was to attain air superiority over the battlefield so that their bombers could give full support to the men attacking on the ground.

The battle these two sides were waging was one for bureaucratic turf and would be won by those who could make the largest claims – whether or not they were realistic. So it proved that the bombardment faction, whose fantasies demanded big bombers that would have to be paid for by big slices of the budgetary pie, and whose arguments made great newspaper headlines, won the battle for control of Air Corps' doctrine. As usual with military mistakes, truth was overwhelmed by optimism.

Chennault, perhaps biased in view of his being a fighter pilot himself, took the side of pursuit, and waged war vigorously. To help get his point across he wrote a new manual for pursuit tactics that was used at the Tactical School, basing his opinions on a study of the aerial tactics of World War I. For prac-

LEFT: A young Claire Chennault in 1917, pictured shortly after joining the army.

BELOW: Chennault's hard-earned wings, finally won in 1919, together with one of his flight books.

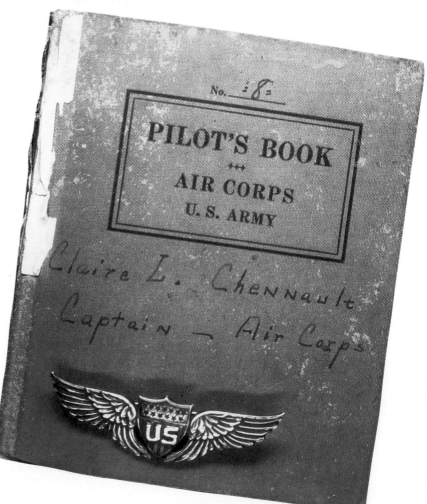

TOP: Chennault's 'Flying Trapeze' specialized in tight formation flying and daredevil maneuvering. It was all to a purpose: to help perfect a systematic approach to fighter combat.

ABOVE: Chennault (center) with 'Flying Trapeze' pilots Mcdonald (left) and Williamson (right).

tical experience he got the Air Corps to set up an aerobatics team, known as 'The Three Men on a Flying Trapeze,' that could test tactical theories as well as provide publicity for the corps by performing at air shows and state fairs. The stunt team always put on a good show of tight formation flying, usually with Chennault himself in the lead aircraft.

Chennault's studies of air combat during World War I, and his practical experience at testing theories and maneuvers with the Flying Trapeze team, helped him to establish the tactical theories that he was to drill the AVG in. The Air Corps' three-plane 'vee' formation was too unwieldy for fast-paced aerial combat and a looser two-plane element was preferable. Surprise was the most

valuable asset a fighter pilot could bring to combat, and aggressive flying, with a pilot figuring out the next attacking move to make, helped to gain or keep the initiative. Getting to close range made it easier to hit the enemy, while concentrating one's fire on the vital areas of the target plane made every shot count, leaving more ammunition for the next victim. By holding the advantage in altitude and speed, a pilot could keep control of the fight. The approach to the target should always be from the best direction – where it had the least armament.

Chennault also emphasized the importance of teamwork in combat. Both pilots were better protected if they flew together, and working with a partner would also make better use of each aeroplane's individual firepower: a good shot for one was often just as good for the other. With teamwork went flexibility: a good pilot instinctively knew when the textbook solution didn't apply, and knew when to trust to his own gut feelings. And finally, Chennault was aware of the value of the old maxim, 'He who fights and runs away, lives to fight another day.' When outnumbered, the best thing a pilot could do was to dive and run, firing one or two well-aimed bursts as a Parthian shot.

Skeptics of Chennault's faith in the fighter conceded that his tactical rules were good, but questioned whether they would be any use, pointing out that fighters still had to find the bombers in a sky that was a good hiding place simply because of its vastness.

Air Raid Warning Net

During maneuvers in Hawaii in 1925, Chennault had stationed some men with binoculars atop the control tower of his air base. They were to scan the skies to give early warning of any approaching aircraft. The time gained would help his fighters to make their interceptions. This was the beginning of Chennault's air raid warning network.

In 1933 he formulated a theory, part of his treatise on fighter tactics. An observation network would be able to keep fighter squadrons informed of the direction, height and size of enemy formations, giving defenders time to match their approach, and attack the intruders on equal terms. Its practicality was first demonstrated that year during maneuvers held at Fort Knox.

Chennault was able to put his theories into practice in China. During the fighting in the Yangtze valley in 1937-8 he had a radio installed in every third Chinese fighter. Concentric circles of trained spotters using the limited telephone and telegraph facilities in the area reported the approach of bombers. The information was plotted on maps at central headquarters. An accurate picture of the approach was created, and the fighters were scrambled. The warning net also gave civilians in the likely targets time to take cover.

A more fully developed version was set up in Yunnan, protecting Kunming. Spotters with radios were sited at listening posts across the province. Some could only be reached by mules; others had to be supplied by air. A clock system was used to indicate the direction of approach, with 12 o'clock being due north. There were also codes for giving altitude, type and number of planes. In 1944 American pilots expressed astonishment at the primitiveness of the net, even though it worked. It was rather tactless since the Chinese had lots of men, but no radar sets.

RIGHT, TOP TO BOTTOM: AVG pilots with one of their P-40s – Eric Shilling; 'Skip' Adair; and Shilling and Bill Bartling on the nose, Joe Rosbert and 'Pappy' Paxton on the wing, and Charlie Bond beneath Shilling.

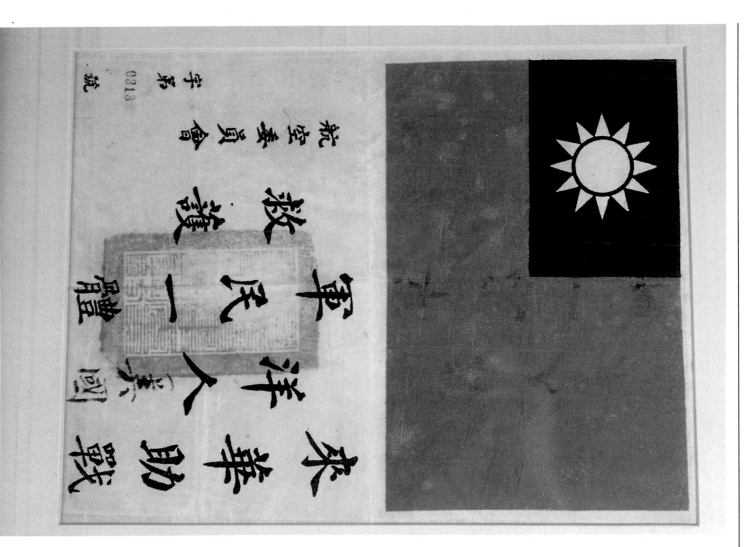

ABOVE: A blood chit as sewn on the back of AVG pilots' uniforms. Its Chinese characters say who it belongs to and what their blood type is. They were instituted to help downed pilots make their way back.

RIGHT: A Hell's Angel beckons from the breast of a 3rd Squadron member's jacket.

BELOW: The original Flying Tigers' patch, with the winged tiger soaring out of a 'vee' for victory.

Chennault, a practical man in his approach to problem solving, had a ready riposte. A network of observers in the forward lines could telephone warnings to fighter bases at the approach of bombers. They could give a good idea of the course being flown and the altitude, as well as the number of aircraft. The pursuit pilots, now alerted, could get into the air and to altitude in time to intercept. Some proof of the practicality of Chennault's warning network was provided by exercises held at Fort Knox in May 1933. During the exercise a majority of the 'enemy' bomber formations were intercepted, but the Air Corps high command was not all that impressed. The lesson they drew was that the enemy fighter bases would have to be bombed first, to put them out of action. The bomber would then get through as a matter of course.

Chennault's souring relationship with his superiors came to a head in November 1935. He was summoned to testify before a commission studying the role of military aviation and the War Department put pressure on all those so summoned to stick to the departmental line. Peacetime armed forces are bureaucratic institutions, ones in which it is better to be safe than right, but Chennault, with the loyalty to his principles and beliefs that marks the man of honor, if not necessarily the one of fame and fortune, was frank before the commission. His testimony was observed by an Air Corps general, who demanded a right to reply on the spot, such was the controversy generated by Chennault.

Chennault paid the price for his honor. His name had appeared on a schedule of officers intended to take a course at the Command and General Staff School at Fort Leavenworth, a course that was a ticket to higher command, but when the new schedule was published in 1936 the name Chennault was, coincidentally, no longer on it. At the age of 42 Chennault had to accept that he had reached the pinnacle of his career in the Air Corps. He did not have the right background for promotion, and perhaps his testimony to the commission has a whiff of burning bridges about it: Chennault realized the limits he faced and was getting in some last licks before departing the service. His family was aware of his plans to retire from the corps in 1937, when he would have served for 20 years.

A chance meeting at a Miami air show in December 1935 provided Chennault with his lucky break. The Curtiss-Wright Aircraft Company's sales agent for China invited Chennault and the Flying Trapeze aboard his yacht. Was Chennault interested in helping the Chinese Air Force? Negotiations began, and in July 1936 Chennault received a formal offer from the Chinese Commission on Aeronautical Affairs giving him charge of fighter pilot instruction for two years on a salary of $12,000 per year.

Chennault's outdoorsman's life and toil in the Tactical School's disputations were taking their toll of his health, and he was in and out of hospital during the winter of 1936-7 suffering from bronchitis. His hearing was also deteriorating. On 25 February 1937, the Air Corps Retirement Board recommended that he leave the service and Chennault, with China beckoning, graciously accepted. At once he received several job offers from American aircraft manufacturers to represent them as a sales agent but he turned them down, choosing to stick with the exotic foreign adventure presented by China. Perhaps he also believed it would give him the opportunity to prove his detractors in the Air Corps wrong. Chennault was retired from active service on 30 April 1937, and sailed for China eight days later.

China could have been on another world for all the resemblance it bore to the bureaucratic, modern Air Corps he had spent his life serving. The facilities available he regarded as of little use in war, while he found that pilot training was strongly influenced by Oriental notions of 'face' and Chiang Kaishek's own need to keep his subordinates happy: no pilot washed out of flight training, the pass record was 100 percent – a pretty remarkable feat for an air force that had only been in existence for the comparatively short time of five years.

BELOW: Chennault, in civilian clothes, with a Chinese officer and two Americans shortly after he had arrived in China in 1937.

ABOVE: Madame Chiang, holding bouquet, was the most important patron the American Volunteer Group had. Her English was spoken with a strong Southern accent which endeared her to the Louisianan Chennault.

Chennault was already planning his first moves in reorganizing pilot training when he visited the air base at Loyang in early July. Then fighting broke out between the Japanese and Chinese. Chiang Kai-shek began deploying his troops for battle, but only on ground of his own choosing. In August he moved the bulk of his best troops to the Shanghai area. An incident was provoked when Chinese troops shot and killed a Japanese naval officer, and by 13 August fighting was underway in earnest, with Japanese ships shelling the docks and harborfront warehouses. Chennault's pilots went into action the next day, as four of the Chinese Air Force's Northrop 2EC light bombers attempted unsuccessfully to sink the flagship of Japan's China fleet, the *Izumo*, moored in the Yangtze roadstead.

Chennault ran the air war for the next few months, forced to battle before he was ready. He did the best he could, and the Chinese were certainly eager to learn. One pilot, returning from action, smashed up his plane. He pulled one of its machine guns from the wreckage, walked over to Chennault and asked, 'Can I have a new plane to go with my machine gun, sir?' Chennault would take his men aside after they had returned from a mission to give them more schooling and he also passed on the benefit of his own observations of Japanese bombing formations and tactics, gleaned from standing out in the streets watching the skies while the target city was under attack. The Japanese were sending their bomber formations into the attack without escorts, and Chennault was able to analyze their weaknesses and instruct his pilots to take advantage of them. It was not long before the Japanese only bombed targets that were within the range of their fighter escorts. Chennault's support for China, and

for his pilots, also extended to flying discreet combat missions of his own. This was in complete violation of America's Neutrality Act and should have cost him his citizenship.

Chennault's one great victory of the Sino-Japanese War came on 29 April 1938. It was Emperor Hirohito's official birthday and Chennault expected that the Japanese would honor it by sending a large raid to bomb one of China's cities. He assembled almost every fighter available to the Chinese Air Force, and made arrangements with a large Soviet contingent that was fighting on behalf of Chiang Kai-shek's regime. Sure enough, a large raid was sent up to bomb Hankow. The Chinese fighters engaged it over the city and the Japanese pilots had to abandon their mission. On their way home they were ambushed by the Soviet fighters. Despite this ray of hope, Chennault's actual successes were limited by a lack of aircraft. Most of China's air force was destroyed in battle or on the ground by the end of 1938. Japan could and did bomb Chinese cities in the south and west with impunity. Chungking, where Chiang Kai-shek's government was headquartered, received particularly heavy raids that left Chennault impressed by the resilience of the Chinese people.

When the United States began to show interest in expanding its aid to China during 1940, Chennault began to develop proposals for organizing a force of American pilots to fly modern planes against the Japanese. On 30 November the Chinese passed on a plan for 500 planes, piloted by US fliers, to the Roosevelt administration's main mover of American aid to countries fighting the Axis powers, Secretary of the Treasury Henry Morgenthau. Morgenthau and the other pro-intervention members of the Roosevelt administration were delighted and studied the proposals in depth under conditions of utmost secrecy. However, when army Chief-of-Staff George C Marshall found out he rounded on the proposal vigorously and stipulated that any US aid to the Chinese Air Force be limited to transferring 100 fighters.

Chennault, now in Washington, expanded the Marshall plan by suggesting that the fighters be flown by volunteers drawn from the Air Corps and the US Navy's carrier squadrons. He had already met with Navy Secretary Frank Knox, who had suggested sending pilots to China in a memorandum to Secretary of State Cordell Hull in October. Both men were probably influenced by the examples of Germany's Condor Legion and the Soviet pilots who fought in the Spanish Civil War. Convinced that sooner or later America would be

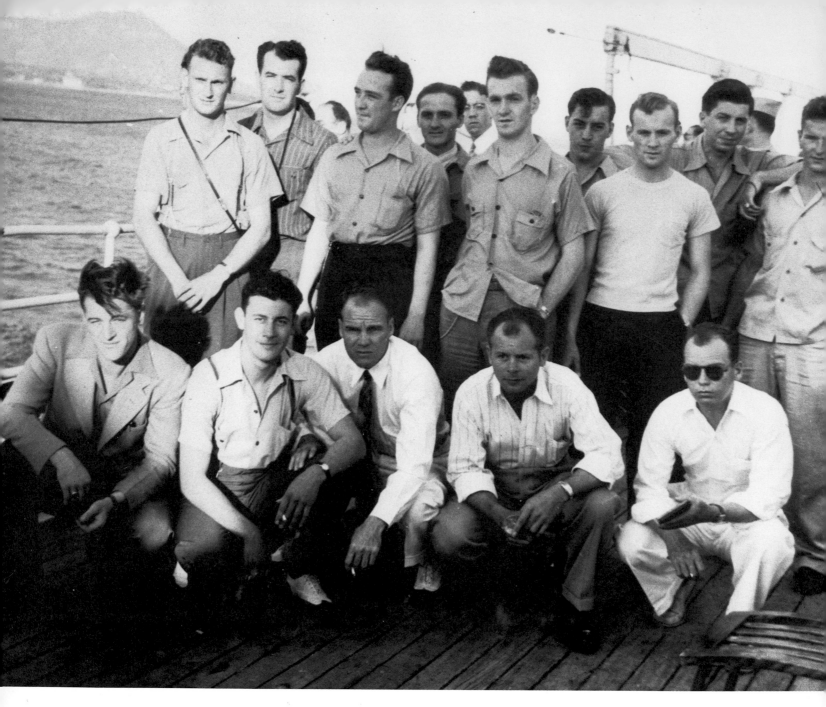

drawn into the war, they reasoned that flying for China would be one way of giving US pilots combat experience.

State, Navy and War Departments all gave approval to Chennault's scheme. To escape violating any neutrality laws, all volunteers would be employed as advisers to the Central Aircraft Manufacturing Corporation (CAMCO). CAMCO would be permitted to send a force of recruiters on tours of US naval and army air bases, offering contracts to trained and commissioned pilots. The criteria Chennault set were for trained fliers aged between 22 and 28. In return for their services the pilots would receive pay of $600 per calendar month for officers, $750 for squadron commanders; mechanics and ground crew received between $350 and $400 a month. A bonus of $500 would be paid for each Japanese plane shot down.

The team of recruiters hit the bases in late March 1941. They had mixed results. Fighter pilots were in very short supply and the Air

Corps was especially reluctant to let any of its trained manpower go. At Hamilton Field the recruiting team were threatened with the guardhouse if they did not get off the field. Most of those encouraged to attend the recruitment meetings by their superiors were hard cases – people with drinking problems, financial worries – pilots whose general attitudes to service life were those of life's nonconformists. Air Corps officers treated those who did sign on with the AVG as little better than deserters. Some refused to accept their men's resignations, but they were asked to telephone or telegraph a Washington, DC, number, and were discreetly informed that it would be in the interest of the United States if they relented and let their men go.

The navy was far more receptive. The recruiters usually had a hangar or a large room allocated to them, and a senior officer would introduce the sales pitch. The difference was reflected in the final figures of pilots:

ABOVE: Members of the AVG on their way to China. Their civilian clothes reveal the private enterprise that the American Volunteer Group legally was. The pilots and ground crew were mercenaries fighting for an ideal, not soldiers performing a duty.

BELOW: Pilots and their wives say their farewells on the deck of the *Jagersfontein.* Jack and Mrs Newkirk are in the center.

BOTTOM: Newly-assembled P-40s in Burma. President Roosevelt himself had exerted his influence with the British to get these planes for Chiang Kai-shek's air force. Originally they had been part of the lend-lease package between Britain and the United States.

more than half came from the navy, the Air Corps contributed 40 percent and the rest came from the Marines. The contract these men signed informed them they were subject to summary dismissal for insubordination, habitual use of drugs or drink, illness or injury incurred not in the performance of duties, malingering, or revealing confidential information. The mechanics were sent to Buffalo to take an intensive course on the Allison inline engine.

The AVG's members were sent in batches across the Pacific. The first group, the ground crew of the AVG, assembled in San Francisco in June 1941 and sailed aboard the *President Pierce*; the first pilots left in the *Jagersfontein* in July. Part way across the Pacific they were joined by two American cruisers that escorted them as they passed through shipping lanes near the Japanese naval bases among the coral

islands of the central Pacific. Japanese radio had reported their impending departure from San Francisco, with unfavorable comment on what to Japanese eyes must have seemed little better than a band of soldiers of fortune. In August the first group of 'Flying Tigers' disembarked onto the docks of Rangoon, Burma. Their great adventure had begun.

For some 30 young American pilots, the hot and heavy air of a Rangoon August must have given them second thoughts about their decision to fight for China. After all, Rangoon was some distance from the land that employed them, and even farther from that of their Japanese enemies. The man who welcomed them to the Far East might not have inspired a rise in confidence in the wisdom of their decision to volunteer. Claire Chennault was of medium height with a wiry body and a face that showed the effects of flying in aeroplanes with open cockpits – his weather-beaten visage earned him the nickname 'Old Leatherface.' Some of his new charges may have perused his textbook on fighter tactics and strategy, *The Role of Defensive Pursuit*, during their recent careers in the Army Air Corps. Most, however, were unlikely to have known much about him, apart from the fact that he was an American serving as Chiang Kai-shek's aviation adviser. It may not have mattered much though: they had joined the American Volunteer Group to be paid good money and to fight the Japanese.

Chennault sent this first contingent of pilots down the railroad line leading north from Rangoon to an out-of-the-way town

called Toungoo. Here the RAF had kindly agreed to put an airfield with an asphalt runway at the disposal of the volunteers. The RAF airfield at Toungoo, called Kyedaw, was an x-shaped, 4000-foot runway that was abandoned during the monsoon months from June through September when the RAF believed it unfit for European habitation. This was how Chennault described it in his memoirs published after the war: 'The runway was surrounded by a quagmire and pestilential jungle. Matted masses of rotting vegetation carpeted the jungle and filled the air with a sour, sickening smell. Torrential monsoon rains and thunderstorms alternated with torrid heat to give the atmosphere of a Turkish bath. . . . Barracks were new and well-ventilated, but along with the air came every stinging insect in Burma. There were no screens or electric lights, and not a foot of screening to be bought in all Burma.'

Olga Greenlaw was one of only three women members of the AVG. Her husband was the group's operations officer. The insects made quite an impression on her: '. . . all the bugs God created to fly through air or crawl on the ground, floors, walls, ceilings, into your food, down your back, up your legs and into your hair – beetles, lice, spiders, flies and fleas, moths, mosquitoes, centipedes, bedbugs, ticks, and a lot more you never heard of. The place was an entomologist's paradise.'

For over two weeks they sat around, suffering from the heat and the mosquitoes – lots of mosquitoes – and the boredom of cooling their heels in a pitiful backwater where there was little to do. Finally, on 21 August, Chennault arrived, worried by reports of impending mutiny among his now-fractious little band. Chennault met with these men individually and in small groups, and organized the mess service, the poor quality of which had been the main source of dissatisfaction. To keep the men occupied, Chennault organized calisthenics and volleyball games. He put his pilots into small groups that would, in turn, be trained in the style of combat suited to aerial warfare against the Japanese.

The first thing he impressed on his pilots was the value of themselves and their equipment. The AVG would be equipped with 99 P-40Bs that the Chinese had only got because President Franklin Roosevelt had twisted the arms of the British, their original intended recipients. The British reluctantly agreed to the transfer when they were informed how dear the project was to the American president. Chennault explained how the P-40s were an invaluable commodity in the Far East. Modern, top-of-the-line fighters were hard for the Chinese to come by, and trained pilots were also in short supply. These two factors meant that each and every AVG pilot had to place the preservation of his plane and his self before any other consideration. A pilot had to be pretty sure of his kill to make the risk worthwhile. It was the factor that all the other training the pilots would receive was based on.

The training day began at six in the morning. The pilots would assemble in one of Kyedaw's shacks to hear Chennault's lecture. The subject matter of these talks was the enemy's planes, and the strengths and weaknesses of the P-40s. Chennault emphasized that the P-40 was a poor plane to try and out-turn a Japanese fighter. Dogfighting was strictly forbidden. The best tactic would be to gain altitude over the enemy and then dive, making a firing pass

BELOW: A P-40 Warhawk painted in the AVG's color scheme. This aircraft is a part of the Confederate Air Force, a private club that flies vintage airplanes.

WESTERN
UNION

COPY

R. B. WHITE
PRESIDENT

NEWCOMB CARLTON
CHAIRMAN OF THE BOARD

J. C. WILLEVER
FIRST VICE-PRESIDENT

1220

CLASS OF SERVICE		SYMBOLS
This is a full-rate Telegram or Cablegram unless its deferred character is indicated by a suitable symbol above or preceding the address.		DL=Day Letter
		NT=Overnight Telegram
		LC=Deferred Cable
		NLT=Cable Night Letter
		Ship Radiogram

The filing time shown in the date line on telegrams and day letters is STANDARD TIME at point of origin.   Time of receipt is STANDARD TIME at point of destination

KAW80 64 4 EXTRA=RK NEWYORK NY 10 1136A

GUY W ARMSTRONG=

715 EAST B=

DEEPLY REGRET TO INFORM YOU THAT WE HAVE RECEIVED THE
FOLLOWING WIRE TODAY QUOTE AMERICAN CONSULATE, RANGOON,
BURMA, TELEGRAPHED THAT CENTRAL AIRCRAFT MANUFACTURING
COMPANY REQUESTS YOU BE INFORMED JOHN DEAN ARMSTRONG WAS
KILLED IN AIRPLANE CRASH SEPTEMBER 8 AT TOUNGOO BURMA WHIL
MAKING PRACTICE FLIGHT AND THAT YOU IMMEDIATELY NOTIFY
PARENTS SIGNED CORDELL HULL, SECRETARY OF STATE UNQUOTE
LETTER FOLLOWS=
        RICHARD ALDWORTH CENTRAL AIRCRAFT MFG CO
        30 ROCKEFELLER PLAZA NYC.

ABOVE: A telegram bearing grim news for the family of John D Armstrong, the first AVG pilot to be killed in service in a crash.

as you raced through the enemy formation, and then keep going. The lighter Japanese planes would never accelerate fast enough to catch a P-40. High-speed hit and run was Chennault's game plan.

Chennault, with the help of captured flying manuals, was also able to teach the volunteers Japanese tactics. Their pilots, with a deep-seated respect for authority and learning, flew by the book. They rigidly kept formation, following the flight leaders. If the formations were broken, however, they got into trouble, being unable to supply the flexibility to compensate for the change in situation. Bomber pilots were especially fanatical about formation flying and would seek to maintain their correct position, even if their comrades were being shot down around them.

Chennault habitually drew pictures of the Japanese planes on a blackboard. Using colored chalks he would ring the vulnerable points, the blind spots, and show the best angle of attack to be made. Beside the drawings, he would write out the speed, maximum altitude, and probable tactics of the aircraft and their pilots. Once he had finished he would ask his men if they had got it all. Nodding their heads was not good enough. The drawing and the information were erased and each pilot in turn came up to the head of the class to prove that he had learned everything by re-drawing the silhouette, correctly marked for vulnerabilities and blind spots, and writing out all the information about its performance.

After learning theories in the schoolroom, the AVG pilots tried to put them into practice. Chennault led them out to the P-40s,

and they flew around Kyedaw in the two-plane elements that were the basic formation for the AVG. The initial flights with the P-40 were none too popular. Few of the volunteers were Air Corps fighter pilots whom Chennault would have considered ideal. They found the P-40 had a high landing speed of 100mph, and that during take-off an awful lot of torque built up in its structure, which had to be compensated for by keeping the rudder turned hard right; it was an Air Corps joke that you could spot a P-40 pilot by his overdeveloped right leg muscles, the result of constantly depressing the right rudder pedal. Navy pilots had to get used to flying an inline, liquid-cooled engine, instead of the air-cooled radials that were standard on carrier aircraft. A further problem arose from a difference of landing technique. In the navy pilots were trained to make three-point landings with the tail down so that the arrester hook could snag a cable; Air Corps planes kept the tail up and put the main gear down first, then the tail. Chennault could always spot a navy pilot landing by a P-40 bouncing along the runway, the result of trying to land with the tail down.

Chennault observed the results of the classroom instruction from the control tower and would issue instructions over the radio while watching the maneuvers being performed. Once the day's flight training was finished he would take aside the pilots and explain where they had gone wrong, or compliment them on what they had done right. The pilots would have no chance for on-the-job training. The AVG developed its personality over the training period. The men of this military unit dressed in unmilitary fashion: they wore an odd mixture of bush jackets, shorts and jungle boots, and no attempt was made at uniformity. Headgear could range from sunhelmets and peaked hats to garrison caps. Saluting was not required and squadron leaders were only rarely accorded this military courtesy, but Chennault was always saluted.

A few of Chennault's pilots left shortly after arriving. One confessed he had only joined up to get a discharge from the service, and then went off to fly commercial aircraft. More serious was the loss of willing pilots in flying accidents. Three were killed during training. The first, John D Armstrong, died on 18 September when his P-40 collided with another while practicing flying in pairs. Two days later Max Hammer was killed while trying to find Kyedaw during a heavy downpour. Peter Atkinson's P-40 crashed on 25 October when it lost its propeller-governor, causing the propeller to

ABOVE: Three flights of P-40s flying over Toungoo airfield.

LEFT: Ground crewmen Morgan Vaux and Don Rodewald.

ABOVE RIGHT: Mechanic Bill Schaper works on a P-40. The shark's teeth nose job has not yet been painted.

ABOVE, FAR RIGHT: Chennault's car gets some gas.

RIGHT: The communications shack, scene of humdrum but vital work.

over-rev and sending the plane into a steep power dive.

Despite these setbacks, the AVG had been turned into a fighting unit by the beginning of December 1941. The last pilots had arrived in the middle of November and were in the final stages of training. Chennault had set up three squadrons and appointed commanders for them. The 1st Pursuit Squadron, nicknamed the 'Adam and Eves' (after the world's first pursuit), was commanded by Texan Robert 'Sandy' Sandell and was made up mainly of former Air Corps pilots. The 'Panda Bears,' the 2nd Pursuit Squadron, was largely a navy outfit, and was headed by John Van Kuren Newkirk, known as 'Scarsdale Jack' after the well-heeled New York City suburb that was his hometown. Army and navy pilots, and a trio of marines christened the 'Three Musketeers' made up the 3rd Pursuit Squadron, 'Hell's Angels,' led by Arvid 'Ole' Olson. The P-40s were now sporting toothy grins along the air intakes of their Allison engines in imitation of similarly painted RAF Tomahawks a couple of the pilots had seen in a magazine.

In the early hours of 8 December 1941, the pilots of the AVG were rousted out of their beds and sent into the air, quickly. The answer to sleepy protests and cries of why was especially alarming to the navy pilots: Pearl Harbor had just been attacked by the Japanese. The AVG was going to war, sooner than it had expected.

THE telephone in the operations room at Kunming airfield in China rang. It was a report that 10 Japanese Army Air force bombers had passed over one of Chennault's warning net stations. The sighting was plotted on the map, and after a couple or more reports, the likely direction of the attack could be guessed at. It was enough to know they were headed toward Kunming. Four planes of the AVG's 2nd Pursuit Squadron, led by Scarsdale Jack Newkirk, took off.

Newkirk and his pilots headed northeastward and about 100 miles from Kunming they made contact with the bombers flying at an altitude of 18,000 feet. Chennault, who had stationed himself in the control tower, heard the report. He ordered his second section, also of four planes, into the air. He also fired a red flare, scrambling 14 more P-40s,

Sandell's flight were surprised to see a lone P-40 still buzzing around the retiring bombers. They didn't watch Rector's display for too long, taking up position for a beam attack. Two flights were positioned to come out of the sun, while the remaining flight and the AVG formation's two tail-end weavers hung back and above. Bob Neale, one of the pilots involved in the action, recalled the day's work later:

'We were flying along above solid overcast when we spotted the 10 bombers. They were lost in soup and trying to get back to Hanoi. They were going like the devil just above the top of the overcast when we saw them. They couldn't have been more than 30,000 feet above the ground. Evidently they had jettisoned their bombs to get more speed. When they spotted us, they put their noses down and ran hell-bent for election.

CHAPTER 3

FIRST SKIRMISHES

this batch under Sandy Sandell. Newkirk was ordered to return to the airfield and act as a combat air patrol, while the second section, led by Jim Howard, covered the city of Kunming itself.

Newkirk did not obey his orders right away. First, the aggressive former navy pilot led his men into a shallow dive through the Japanese formation. Chennault's iron rule of keeping in pairs was broken as each P-40 made a separate run. The Japanese bombers, Mitsubishi Ki-27s, jettisoned their bombs and the shallow 'V' formation began a slow turn round to head back for home. Newkirk's flight opened fire as they dived, but the bombers were out of range of their guns. Three of the four P-40s turned back to Kunming, but the fourth pilot, Ed Rector, wasn't giving up so easily. He chased the bombers for as long as he could, but eventually ran out of fuel and had to crash-land in a rice paddy. He had lost a valuable plane without bringing an enemy bomber down.

We chased them for about 10 minutes before we caught them. Sandell sailed in first with the assault echelon, and I followed with my reserve flight. Bob Little stayed above with the support echelon to cover our attack.

'We went in in rat-race formation, everybody chasing the tail of the plane ahead. We opened fire, and the bombers seemed to fall into pieces. I saw pieces of engine cowling fall off into space. Glass from the gun turrets flew in all directions. Engines smoked and caught fire. Tails just crumped and fell off. It was the queerest thing I ever saw. Then the air was so full of P-40s dashing all over the place that I worried more about colliding with a P-40 than about the Japs.'

Sandell's planes dogged the Japanese for 100 miles, before they finally broke off their attacks, running low on fuel and ammunition. One pilot, Fritz Wolf, brought down two bombers:

'I attacked the outside bomber in a V. Diving down below him, I came up under-

LEFT: Japanese bombers over Rangoon.

neath, guns ready for the minute I could get in range. At 500 yards I let go with a quick burst from all my guns. At 100 yards I let go with a long burst that tore into the bomber's gas tanks and engine. A wing folded and a motor tore loose. Then the bomber exploded. I yanked back on the stick to get out of the way and then went upstairs.

'Then I went after the inside man. I came out of a dive and pulled up level with the bomber just behind his tail. I could see the rear gunner blazing away at me but none of his bullets were hitting my plane. At 50 yards I let go with one long burst, concentrating on one motor . . . the bomber burned and then blew up.'

Wolf was lining up a shot on a third when he pressed the triggers only to find his guns were empty. Although the first two runs were made in pairs, just as Chennault had recommended, toward the end of their work the AVG were making single attacks, hitting the formations from all directions. Sandell, in his combat report, reckoned that his men had brought down six of the bombers. Other observers, claiming to have sighted the Japanese formation as it returned to its base at Hanoi, said that all but one of the bombers had crashed on the flight back. However many it actually was, there was no doubt that the AVG had won its first victory.

On the morning of 8 December, Chennault had been fearful that the Japanese would hit Toungoo in a surprise attack. When sunset came, and the day ended with no sign of enemy air activity, he was relieved. But he also ordered preparations for a photo-reconnaissance mission to be flown over the main Japanese air base at Bangkok. The unarmed P-40 with its cameras, and two standard P-40s flying escort, took off on the 11th. The photographs it took revealed Don Muang airfield to be jam-packed with enemy aircraft. After seeing the pictures, Chennault chose to withdraw the majority of the AVG to Kunming. There was no warning net around Toungoo similar to that at Kunming, and he believed the airfield too close to Japanese bomber bases for comfort.

Chennault would have liked to have withdrawn the whole of his command, but he didn't get his way. Part of the deal for training the AVG at Kyedaw was that if Burma was attacked, the AVG would help with its air defense. British commanders hoped for the whole of the AVG to be stationed at Mingaladon, the main RAF base outside of Rangoon. There were sound reasons for the British hopes. With all of China's seaports in the hands of the Japanese, the only way for military supplies to reach China was along the winding road from Lashio to Paoshan

ABOVE: Ed Rector poses for the camera while getting into his P-40.

LEFT: 'Doc' Richards beside the group's ambulance.

TOP: AVG and British pilots swap stories at Mingaladon.

ABOVE: AVG P-40s fly over the arid terrain of southwestern China.

RIGHT: George Cuvvan armed with a revolver and plenty of ammunition, stands beside the AVG's ambulance.

through the mountains of Yunnan, known as the Burma Road. Rangoon provided the transshipment point as matériel was unloaded from ships and driven on trucks down to Lashio. If Rangoon were to fall to the Japanese, then all aid to China would have to be flown into the country.

Chennault, however, was concerned at the inefficiencies he believed afflicted Rangoon's early warning system. Although the RAF had a radar set, and radar had been invaluable for the defense of Britain during the summer of 1940, the information about approaching aircraft would have to be transmitted over a notoriously unreliable telephone and telegraph network; there were no secure military lines of communication. Chennault's reservations were overruled by the desire of Chiang Kai-shek to prove China a capable and contributing ally: he was ordered to provide a squadron of the AVG for the defense of Rangoon. So Chennault sent the 1st and 2nd Pursuit Squadrons to Kunming, while the 3rd Hell's Angels Squadron flew the short hop to Mingaladon. Sandell managed to get his 1st Pursuit Squadron over the mountainous Burma-China border using only a topographical map for guidance.

While the Adam and Eves and Panda Bears were knocking Japanese bombers attacking Kunming out of the sky, the Hell's Angels were waiting tensely for the first Japanese blow against Rangoon. It was certain to come. Burma had great value for the 'Greater East Asia Co-Prosperity Sphere' that was the ultimate purpose of Japan's decision to go to war. It was a country rich in minerals and rice, and holding it would also seal Chiang Kai-shek's regime off from the world and make its eventual defeat inevitable. It also would provide an excellent buffer against attacks from India as Burma's road network and railroad system were not well developed and the countryside was rugged. It would be difficult for a modern army to cross it, and Tokyo would have ample warning if the British were to try penetrating the defensive perimeter, giving time for reinforcements to be moved from the homeland before they got close to more valuable regions such as the East Indies.

Any Japanese attempt to take Burma, however, was delayed by the need to secure Thailand. The Fifteenth Army was given both tasks. Taking over Thailand would occupy it fully for several weeks and any Japanese attacks on the Allies in Burma in the meantime would have to be made by the Army Air Force's 10th Air Brigade.

Rangoon had already suffered two false alarms on 23 December, when the air raid sirens' mournful wail went off again at 1100 hours. The difference this time was that the wail was punctuated by the explosions of anti-aircraft shells. Chennault's fears were confirmed as neither the Hell's Angels nor the RAF's No 67 Squadron got up in time to stop the first wave of 18 Ki-27 bombers from dropping their loads on Rangoon's docks. A second wave of 30 bombers was not so lucky; heading for Mingaladon they were set upon by an angry swarm of 16 P-40s and 20 RAF Buffaloes. While the RAF pilots tangled with the 20 fighter escorts, the AVG pilots tore into the bomber formation. A pair of two-plane teams made the first diving passes, swinging in from the flanks. The leader of one team, Robert 'Tadpole' Smith came through the crossfire from the bombers and leveled off on the rear bomber's tail. He opened fire at a range of 50 feet, his first burst setting the target's wing tanks on fire. As the wing burned up, the bomber lost altitude, then began a long, slow dive to the ground. Charlie Older picked the formation leader for his target. Sharp shooting hit the bomber in the bomb bay, blowing it up. He then began to make head-on passes at the formation, pouring fire from his guns into the bomber's radial engines.

The bombers droned on, seemingly oblivious to these attacks, dropping their payloads in the vicinity of Mingaladon. Parker Dupouy, one of the Hell's Angels' flight leaders, led four planes in a head-on pass, while Neil Martin led another in a right-flank attack. Although neither pass resulted in a kill, the formation now began to straggle, a sign that the targets had been badly damaged. Ken Jernstedt blew up another bomber, while Bob Hedman, who dove through the fighter cover to get at the targets, drilled a 10-second burst into one, making very sure of his kill.

But there were losses to the AVG too. Neil Martin's aircraft hurtled through the bomber formation at the same time that Charlie Older's bullets found the bomb bay of the Japanese leader. Martin may have been hit by fire from the bomber's guns, or the concussions resulting from the explosion of the bomber may have damaged the controls of the plane; the P-40 tumbled out of the sky and crashed, killing its pilot.

Henry Gilbert and Paul Greene were attacking some of the formation's stragglers when they were bounced by six Type 97 fighters. The pair had claimed one bomber when four of the Japanese fighters made swooping passes on Gilbert's P-40, riddling it. It crashed, and Gilbert did not survive. Greene was a little luckier. Set upon by two

fighters, he was forced to bail out. After his parachute had opened and he was floating back to earth, the fighters came back to finish him. As they made their passes, Greene would spill his 'chute so that he was tossed first one way, then the other. Eventually he became so tired that he could spill no longer. He chose instead to just hang from the harness, playing opossum. It worked but the canopy of his parachute was so badly shot up that he landed hard, jarring his back.

On the flight back to Mingaladon, the Hell's Angels noticed one of their number missing. Hedman was keen to become an ace. As well as his victim of the 10-second burst, he had got another bomber and two fighters. He now dogged the retreating bomber formation across the Gulf of Martaban, cleverly flying in the center so that the gunners could only shoot at him if they were prepared to risk damaging one of their comrades. Choosing his shot with the care that marked the way he usually did things, Hedman singled out the leader of the formation for his fifth kill of the day, becoming an ace after only his first air battle.

Once the AVG had landed their ground crews raced to ready the planes in case the

ABOVE: Parker Dupouy (right) with one of the AVG's radiomen. Dupouy was one of the 3rd Squadron's flight leaders.

ABOVE: RAAF Brewster Buffaloes. Finnish pilots had flown them to several victories against Soviet fliers in the 1939-40 Winter War, but by the time British, American and Australian airmen began using them against the Japanese, they had been modified and made too heavy for their powerplant. Buffaloes made up most of the RAF's fighter squadrons in Burma.

RIGHT: Duke Hedman, of the 3rd Squadron, became an ace in a single day of combat.

FAR RIGHT: AVG ace 'Tadpole' Smith contemplates just how far away from home he is.

Japanese should launch another raid. Several trucks had been converted to make mobile servicing units for the planes. One, for example, had been fitted with gas tanks so that it could race across the field from plane to plane, topping up their tanks. Another had all the tools and spare parts necessary for repairing the engines. There was another with the equipment and extra ammunition needed to recharge the guns. A fourth carried oxygen supplies to top up the bottles in the cockpit. The vehicles were the brainchild of the Hell's Angels' line chief, the man with the responsibility for running the squadron's ground crews. Glen Blaylock had put his men through rigorous training to get the best out of these units, and it paid off. They proved so useful that they were left behind at Mingaladon when the Hell's Angels were rotated out, to be used by the other two squadrons when they did their part in the defense of the embattled capital of Burma.

In the event, on 23 December the AVG

LEFT: With a bent propeller and a malfunctioning engine, P-40 number 67 is given a tow back to the hangar.

BELOW: A P-40 taxis along the airstrip at Mingaladon.

ABOVE: The Silver Grill in Rangoon, where the rambunctious behavior of the AVG pilots so disturbed the reserve of Burma's colonial elite. Once Japanese bombs had started to fall on the city, however, the American pilots' presence as part of the city's defense force was more welcome.

was a very large bomber formation, headed toward Rangoon. Estimates of the size of this force ranged up to 84 bombers, escorted by 42 fighters. Olson received this grim news, and sent his pilots into the air. The squadron's 12 P-40s were divided into two flights of six planes each.

The Japanese were grouped into three distinct waves. The first AVG flight, with George McMillan at the front, hit the first wave of attackers hard – Older, Tom Haywood and Hedman each claimed a bomber. Another five also crashed, but before the AVG could pause the second wave was upon them. Hedman added three more vic-

needn't have readied their aircraft for a return engagement. The Japanese were finished for the day. They would be back, however. The upper echelons of Rangoon society, the colonial administrators and businessmen who were the feature of any of the major cities of Britain's empire, looked a little less sour when the Flying Tigers turned up at the Silver Grill, where one or two stiff upper lips had quivered at the sight of rowdy, shabbily-dressed Americans noisily calling out for doubles, brazenly wearing handguns on their hips, and generally lowering the tone of what had been a pretty respectable place for a civilized drink. That evening the regulars at the Silver Grill were pleased to see the AVG having a far from quiet drink with their RAF counterparts. After all, 25 Japanese planes had been turned into wrecks because of the pilots' actions that day.

Christmas Eve passed quietly, but the AVG was on its toes for Christmas Day. Olson had been disappointed at the lateness of the warning he had received and this time had a patrol up to keep a look out for any Japanese attacks. What they had to report

Going Downtown in 1942

While the Japanese were hammering Rangoon, Chennault decided to mount a small raid against their main air base in Indochina, at Hanoi. Eighteen Soviet-supplied SB-3 bombers of the Chinese Air Force were moved to Kunming, and planning for the raid began.

Hanoi was at the extreme range of the bombers, and the P-40s that would fly escort would have to refuel somewhere along the way. Navigation would also be difficult because of a lack of check stations en route.

The first raid was made on 22 January. The bombers loaded up with all the bombs they could, then took off from Chang Yi, an airfield north of Kunming. The rendezvous with their P-40 escorts from the AVG went off all right and the formation flew southeast. The P-40s had to stop and refuel at Mengtsz, while the bombers plodded on, and then catch up again with their charges. The AVG pilots knew they were above Hanoi when the sky was peppered with anti-aircraft bursts around them. The SB-3s dropped their bombs, but how the bombardiers could aim them at a height above the cloud deck was a mystery to the fighter pilots. Both the P-40s and the SB-3s got safely home. There was no lasting damage to the Japanese airfield.

A second raid was attempted the next day. The same routine was followed, but this time one bomber was lost to anti-aircraft fire, and another had to make a forced landing in Indochina with engine trouble. The Viet Minh, anti-Japanese nationalists led by Ho Chi Minh, helped the Chinese to hide the plane and get repairmen to fix it. The mended SB-3 was successfully flown off and returned to China.

tims to take his tally for the two days of fighting to nine, but his luck almost ran out. Four Japanese fighters caught him as he dived away on his last pass. The bullets of their 7.7mm guns shattered the glass of his canopy, and the last thing their pilots saw was Hedman slumped over the controls of his battered plane. He was not dead, though, and managed to get his damaged plane back to Mingaladon.

McMillan had shot up a bomber on his first pass, then spotted a straggler heading back for Thailand over the Gulf of Martaban. He closed the range to 10 feet before he was ready to open fire, when the bomber's tail gunner opened up on him, shooting off his bulletproof windshield and knocking out the cooling equipment of his engine. McMillan had to dive away and head back to Rangoon. Bob Smith made a climbing pass on his victim and the bullets from his machine hit the bomb bay, causing the bomber to explode. His engine cowling was peppered with fragments of the cylinder heads.

The other flight was led by Parker Dupouy. Examining the combat reports of 23 December Dupouy, McMillan and Olson had concluded that the Japanese fighters, mostly Type 97s, lacked the speed to catch up with the bombers they escorted if they stopped to mix it with attacking fighters. The Americans concluded that if they tangled briefly with the escorts, they could then dive away and, using their superior speed, catch up with the bombers, leaving the escorts some distance behind. Dupouy's flight tangled briefly with the second wave's escorts before making its diving passes on the bombers. In the action with the fighters, Fred Hodges claimed one victim. Dupouy lined up a shot behind a Japanese fighter only to watch it turn away at the last instant. However, as the Japanese fighter rolled his plane, his wing struck the wing of Dupouy's P-40. The sturdier construction of the American product was proven: the Japanese plane's wing was shorn off, while Dupouy's aircraft had only lost four feet of a wingtip. The Japanese crashed into the sea, while Dupouy was able to land his P-40 back at Mingaladon.

Bob Brouk and Lewis Bishop also attempted to land at Mingaladon during the fight. They had heard an order to 'pancake' - the codeword to land at once – over their radios and made their way back to the field. However, as they were coming in Japanese fighters appeared, machine guns blazing. Brouk and Bishop had to quickly abort their intended landing, and were furious at the control tower for giving such an irresponsible order with Japanese planes about. The

men in the control tower insisted they were innocent, and showed the log of messages to prove their case. English-speaking Japanese pilots had overheard the codeword while listening in the Allied fighter frequencies. They then hung around Mingaladon, while broadcasting a phony order to land. Brouk and Bishop were the unwitting victims of this subterfuge, but luckily were able to escape.

The rest of his flight rejoined their leader, except for Ed Overend. Overend had made four passes at the Japanese formations before shortage of fuel forced him to crash-land in a rice paddy. He was surrounded by peasants who shouted angrily and waved their sickles at the downed flier. Fortunately Overend, a Californian, was a born wheeler-dealer. His comrades knew him as someone who was always ready to make a deal with the locals, swapping lighters and similar odds and ends for souvenirs or food. He was able to demonstrate to the peasants' satisfaction that he was really on their side.

The fighting had lasted an hour and a half. All of the Hell's Angels returned safely to

ABOVE: Two of the men who kept the P-40s in the air: 1st Squadron line chief J J Harrigan and mechanic Preston Paul.

RIGHT: Ed Overend, AVG ace and wheeler-dealer.

BELOW: Ground crew of the 2nd Squadron. These men worked under difficult conditions. By day they hauled the P-40s about the field, and rushed to the aid of any that had crash-landed near Mingaladon. By night they worked hard to repair the damage of the day's battles.

Mingaladon except for McMillan and Over-end. Overend's rough landing was reported, and he turned up later in the day. McMillan's loss was deeply felt, however. The arrival of a Christmas treat – a truckload of ham, chicken, cold beer and whiskey, the gift of CAMCO's chief executive William Pawley, then visiting Rangoon – went a little way to cheering them up. The pilots of the AVG had, before then, staved off hunger with warm beer and stale bread. They were cheered up even more the next day by the return of McMillan, in the back of a bullock cart. His fighter had been too badly damaged to make it back to Rangoon and he had to bail out over the jungles that surrounded the city. McMillan had spent Christmas night wandering through the forest trying to find a way back to his comrades, who were then toasting the day's success with Pawley's Christmas gift. McMillan's wandering had come to an end when he chanced upon the bullock cart, whose driver agreed to take him back to Mingaladon.

The Christmas Day fighting had netted another 13 kills for the AVG's pilots. Their run of success moved squadron leader Olson to telegraph Chennault back at Kunming: 'LIKE SHOOTING DUCKS STOP WOULD PUT ENTIRE JAP FORCE OUT OF COMMISSION WITH GROUP HERE STOP . . . .' Damage to aircraft and the loss of four planes had reduced the Hell's Angels number of serviceable fighters to 11, however, and the war was only just beginning. Chennault had seen those photographs of the Thai airfields packed with Japanese aircraft and, rather than use up all of the squadron's precious aircraft, he decided to rotate them out of Rangoon and replace them with the 2nd Pursuit Squadron. The Hell's Angels had done their bit.

NEW Year's Day was marked by the AVG with an arrival and a departure: the Hell's Angels left Rangoon and the Panda Bears arrived. The Panda Bears were already veterans of combat, having contributed to the victory at Kunming 11 days before. The Panda Bears had the reputation of being the most boisterous of the three AVG squadrons, and the bulk of its pilots had been in the navy, including squadron leader Jack Newkirk. Newkirk no doubt provided a suitable role model for the pilots and men of the Panda Bears; he was full of nervous energy and always looking for action, being inclined to make trouble if he couldn't find it. He had gone to school at Rensselaer Polytechnic Institute, and while a student had been involved in several automobile accidents, the tangible results of his daredeviltry. In the navy he had served as a bomber

fighters had made their passes, they performed an Immelmann (a climbing loop) and came round for a head-on attack.

In a scene resembling the chivalric jousts of the early stages of aerial warfare during World War I, Newkirk and one of the Type 96s raced toward one another with guns blazing. Newkirk's heavy .50 calibers in the P-40's fuselage nose gave him an advantage over his opponent's rifle-caliber weapons; he shot the wing off the Japanese plane. As Howard came in for his strafe a pair of Type 96s rode his tail. Tex Hill flew to Howard's rescue, and his bullets found the fuel tank of one of the Japanese fighters. After it had exploded, its comrade flew off. Newkirk, now climbing away from the airfield, found himself once again going head-to-head with a pair of Type 96s, and again he emerged the victor, shooting down one of the attackers.

CHAPTER 4

BATTLE FOR RANGOON

pilot aboard the USS *Yorktown*.

Newkirk's belief in aggressive action was put into practice two days after his squadron's arrival in Rangoon. On 3 January he took off from Mingaladon with Jim Howard and Tex Hill for an offensive reconnaissance of Japanese airfields in Thailand. They flew as far east as Tak, a little over the border, where they spotted an airfield with bombers on the runway. They flew down and strafed the runway a few times and, satisfied with their work, turned for home. The Panda Bears' trio then found another Japanese airfield at Meshod, southwest of Tak. It seemed likely that word of their presence had gotten around, because the ground crews were busy pushing their unit's aircraft off the airfield when the AVG pilots attacked. They made one pass and performed a *chandelle* (a climbing turn), but as they were about to begin their second run, six Type 96 fighters swooped down in a diving attack on their tails. After the Japanese

The remaining three Japanese fighters flew for home, leaving the Panda Bears to make their way back to Mingaladon unhindered.

The Japanese returned the AVG's favor the next day, when a large formation of aircraft appeared on the radar screen. Six of the Panda Bears took off to counter the attackers. They were joined later by eight more P-40s that would fly top cover while the first six flew at a lower altitude of 11,000 feet. The Japanese were coming out of the southeast, flying at 18,000 feet. When they spotted the six P-40s 7000 feet below, they immediately dived to attack. George Paxton was one of the victims of this diving assault:

'We got down to 11,000 feet . . . I looked around one second and the sky was clear. The next second the air was full of little red and silver planes. They dove past us to attack. Ken Merritt on my left peeled off. Hank Geselbracht kept going. My first impulse was to dive off to the left. Then I remembered Chennault's "Always fight in

LEFT: Japanese Type 96 bombers drop their loads over Rangoon.

pairs.'' I reached for the gun switch and all hell broke loose in my cockpit – awful thuds of bullets hitting everything, glass, armor, seats, everything. . . . Things got sort of cloudy.

'I wanted more than anything else to roll over and dive out, but all movement turned to slow motion. . . . The crashing of bullets never seemed to quit. I knew I had been hit – shoulder, leg and arm. They all burned. Somehow I got over into a dive. Then I knew I was spinning. An awful smell of smoke filled the cockpit. . . . Then I was out of the spin and the pounding of the lead stopped. . . . The instrument panel was covered with oil. So was the windshield. . . . I could still work my arms and legs and the controls responded . . . I leveled off. The windshield started to disintegrate.

'I circled in to land and the left side of the windshield fell out when I turned . . . Got the wheels down . . . sat braced for the crash . . . Didn't nose over . . . somebody pulled me out. The doctor gave me some morphine and the burning in my side stopped. I felt pretty good.'

Ground crew counted 61 holes in Paxton's P-40.

Merritt may have dived away initially, but he came back to rescue Paxton, shooting down the Japanese fighter on his tail. Geselbracht also scored a victory, but Bert Christman's P-40 was badly shot up by three of the Japanese fighters. Christman, who had been a cartoonist's assistant on the famous 'Terry and the Pirates' comic strip, managed to bail out safely. A third victim of the battle, in which the pilots faced odds of nearly five to one, was Gil Bright. Bright's plane was riddled with 7.7mm rounds, yet he managed to crash-land it without injury to himself. However, a fire broke out and just as Bright got out of the cockpit a fuel tank blew up. Quite a few of his machine

ABOVE: Tex Hill, with 16 confirmed kills one of the AVG's top aces, describes how it's done. Hill was one of the few Flying Tigers who chose to stay on with Chennault following the disbandment of the AVG.

FAR LEFT: George Paxton in the AVG's full dress uniform.

LEFT: Chennault, Chiang, Madame Chiang and other Chinese dignitaries in front of a 3rd Squadron P-40 at Kunming.

RIGHT: 'Skip' Adair muses over the wreckage of a P-40 crash-landed by George Paxton.

BELOW: Pillars of smoke mark the detonation of Japanese bombs in Rangoon.

guns' rounds cooked off, yet Bright managed to get away with bad burns on his face, but alive.

Curiously, the eight planes flying top cover were completely unaware of the near disaster that had befallen their comrades flying below. They only received news of the fighting after they had landed back at Mingaladon at the end of an uneventful patrol.

The Japanese fighter sweep of 4 January was the first step in a measured offensive against the AVG and the RAF squadrons defending southern Burma. The next day bomber formations converged on Rangoon from three different directions. The Japanese were sending smaller bomber formations that were escorted by much larger numbers of fighters. While the Panda Bears engaged the raiders, more fighters flew in at low level to strafe the Allied airfields.

The air battle for Rangoon launched on 4 January lasted three days. The fighting was fierce and confused. The Panda Bears faced a grueling struggle in the air. Japanese pilots frequently broadcast phony messages such as had tricked Brouk and Bishop on Christmas Day, while Japanese radio transmitters in Thailand attempted to jam the frequencies used by Rangoon's air raid warning spotters. The AVG also had tricks up its own sleeve. Some of its Chinese mechanics constructed dummy aeroplanes out of wood which were left out in the open while the real P-40s were carefully camouflaged and placed on the edges of the airfields. When Japanese fighter planes came in to strafe the AVG's bases, they concentrated their fire on the dummies, leaving their real targets unharmed.

The daylight raids mounted by the Japanese did little harm to Mingaladon, but they suffered many casualties. The Japanese realized the poor exchange they were getting, and the daylight attack launched by them on 6 January was the last such incursion for two weeks. The heavy casualties suffered had taken their toll of the squadrons, reducing their ability to carry out their mission effectively. Another reason for the let-up was the need to conserve aircraft and air crew for the soon-to-be-launched offensive into Burma. The Japanese were well aware of the importance of supporting operations on the ground with air raids on enemy positions.

The aerial attacks that the Japanese did launch over the next two weeks were confined to night time 'wake-up calls' in which a small force, or even a solitary bomber, came over under cover of darkness and dropped bombs in the vicinity – or at least what the pilot and bomb aimer thought was the vicinity – of Mingaladon. Like the daylight raids, these harrassment attacks achieved little real damage, but their nuisance value was profound.

On the night of 8/9 January, three AVG pilots, Jim Howard, Pete Wright and Gil Bright, attempted to intercept one of the night-time intruders with the help of directions from the ground controller. Such a mission was a difficult operation even later in the war when some night fighters were equipped with radar. Doing such an interception in a P-40 with a ground controller and fighter pilots lacking training for it was unlikely to bring success. The attempt to intercept was a failure, and in fact ended in catastrophe. To light the runway for the returning P-40s, the ground crew and pilots had lined up cars and jeeps along the edge of the airstrip. Their headlights were good enough to guide the P-40s, but one of them, piloted by Wright, misjudged the approach and crashed into one of the cars. Three AVG pilots were inside with the radio on. Two of them managed to get away, but the third, Ken Merritt, was asleep in the rear seat. His body was later retrieved from the wreck.

He was the second pilot the Panda Bears had lost in 24 hours. On 8 January four had taken off for a strafing attack on Japanese bases in Thailand – Charlie Mott, Percy Bartelt, Bob Moss and Gil Bright. They hit an airfield near Meshod. Mott tells the story:

BELOW: A camouflaged P-40. Deceptions such as a camouflaged or dummy aircraft saved the AVG's precious planes several times during the fighting in Burma.

ABOVE: During night operations, this car was struck by a P-40 attempting to land. AVG pilot Ken Merritt, who was asleep in the rear of the car, was killed in the accident.

RIGHT: The aftermath of a raid on Mingaladon.

'The Japs were always on the alert at daybreak, which is a favorite time for attack. So I decided that in view of the circumstances, we'd try to catch them at high noon when they were eating lunch. We came roaring down, two of us to strafe and two to fly top cover and get anybody that got off. Lo and behold, there it was in the bright sunlight. There were about four planes in a line, their ready flight. There were a lot of people working on the airfield, extending one end of the runway. We had orders not to, that our war was not with the Thais, though they subsequently declared war on us, and that they were neutral at that time. We caught them right out in the open, literally a couple of hundred of them there, but I couldn't identify them as Japs, so I just fired a burst over their heads and into the planes beyond. We didn't machine gun them.

'The first pass we got those four planes, and then looked round and saw some more planes out in the boonies at the edge of the field camouflaged. We went after them and we got them. We came around in a *chandelle* looking for more and lo and behold a little farther out I spotted a glint of silver and yeah, there was one of them, camouflaged down in the bushes. We came down on him and were about to open fire when something big hit. I was uninjured, but there was a hell of a bang and smoke, and the engine quit cold. I had something over 200 knots at that time.

'So I went through the mechanically "what the hell" process. I turned the stop cock, and flipped the mags, and worked the throttle with absolutely no results. By this time I was beginning to lose air speed so I pulled up, rolled over, kicked myself out, and pulled the rip cord immediately. It seemed to take minutes for that parachute to open. Meanwhile, the ground was rushing up and just before I hit the 'chute blossomed and bango – I went in a tree. That's where I got banged up, with a broken pelvis, broken arm, broken foot, and a few other things.'

Mott was taken prisoner by the Japanese, and went on to Panda Bears' records as missing in action. He survived a Japanese prisoner-of-war camp and was released at the end of the war.

Strafing raids were made almost every day by the Panda Bears in keeping with Newkirk's preference for carrying the war to the enemy. Their frequent presence over Thailand caused the Japanese to institute a system of combat air patrols over their bases. The two-plane strafe with two planes as top cover, described by Mott, enabled even such a protected target airfield to be hit, as the top cover took care of the patrolling fighters.

His pilots also flew escort for RAF Blenheim bombers which made attacks on Japanese troop columns and supply lines. These missions revealed that the Japanese were readying for their thrust into Burma. The fall of Manila in the Philippines in early January had enabled them to reinforce their air strength in Thailand, adding an air bri-

gade to the one already present. The second warning sign of the impending onslaught came when Japanese troops moved forward on 15 January to occupy the airfield at Tavoy in the central section of Burma's panhandle. The British military authorities had hoped to deny this objective to the Japanese for as long as possible, and its early loss in the campaign improved the ability of the Japanese air forces to support the attacks of the soldiers on the ground.

Five days after the Japanese had occupied Tavoy, they crossed the Thai-Burma border in strength. Their initial objective was the capture of Moulmein. The Panda Bears, thanks to damage suffered during their strafing raids, were down to eight ser-

TOP LEFT: Pilot Bob Layher in shorts and Ray Bans beside his aircraft.

TOP: Pilot 'Buster' Keeton (left) with another member of the AVG.

ABOVE: Three Panda Bears – (left to right) Peter Wright, Joe Rosbert and Ed Goyette.

ABOVE: The top AVG ace was Bob Neale.

BELOW: Japanese troops in Burma. While the AVG could fend off any attacks on Rangoon from the air, once the enemy's army neared the Burmese capital, the Flying Tigers had no choice but to abandon it.

viceable aircraft when they received reinforcements from Kunming in the shape of eight pilots and planes from the Adam and Eves in the middle of January. This reinforcement came just in time for the next series of big air battles around Rangoon, as the Japanese once again cranked up the air war.

Early in the morning of the 23rd a large force of Type 97 fighters performed a sweep over Rangoon, concentrating their assault on Mingaladon. The AVG was caught with its pants down. The first planes to take off were piloted by Frank Lawlor and Tex Hill. It was fortunate, given the circumstances, that Lawlor was one of the pair. He was a crack shot, using very little ammunition to score his kills, and had the respect of the whole of the Panda Bears for his marksman's eye. For 10 minutes the two pilots battled the Japanese, despite being outnumbered by almost three to one. Diving or rolling away, they managed to keep out of

the gunsights of the more maneuverable enemy fighters. Lawlor even managed to get one of them on his first pass. On his second he shot another of the lightly built Type 97s to pieces. Finally, five RAF fighters arrived to help out the embattled pair of Panda Bears. These seven were then joined by three more P-40s, piloted by Bob Neale, Bill Bartling and Bob Little. The five Flying Tigers claimed seven kills without loss in this fight.

Just after lunch the Japanese renewed their attack, sending 31 bombers, in two waves of 19 and 12, escorted by 30 fighters. Ten of the AVG's P-40s got into the air. Newkirk's combat report, filed after the action, reveals the character of the fighting:

'When we reached our ceiling we singled out the bombers. We made attacks on them from three directions – dead ahead and on the port and starboard. After several passes the left-hand plane that I was attacking fell out of formation, but staggered back into

life. Then the formation turned. One plane gave several large puffs of smoke and went down near a satellite field. The plane I was following finally went down after several more bursts. I was then attacked by several Type 97 . . . and had to break off.

'One of the fighters dove 3000 feet past me. As he turned to climb back I caught him just over Pegu. After one burst his wing came off. Down he went. Another bunch of fighters had been shooting at me, so I returned to the field.'

The words of the report do not reveal the extent of the damage to his P-40. As Newkirk came in to land, he discovered that during the combat his fighter's flaps had been shot off. Unable to slow his plane sufficiently, he overshot the field and had to crash-land. However, he was undaunted. He got a new P-40 and brought down a couple more Japanese planes that day.

Bob Neale, remembering Chennault's lessons back in Toungoo, came roaring through a Japanese fighter formation to break it up. He claimed one kill for that pass. He then tried the same trick on a bomber formation, and once again was rewarded with a score. Noel Bacon got off the runway later than the other 10 but his aggressive flying paid dividends. He performed a wingover – a climbing turn while rolling the plane in order to reverse its direction of flight – to position himself for a head-on attack against a group of fighters. He got two, but his P-40 was badly shot up in the process, although he managed to get away.

Bert Christman, the cartoonist, was attacked by three Japanese fighters at 12,000 feet. The fire from their 7.7mm machine guns smashed up the Allison inline engine and Christman had to bail out. As he was getting out of the cockpit, one of the Japanese came back and machine-gunned him in the chest, killing him. Christman's partner, Ed Rector, was now out for revenge. He followed Christman's killer, who was making a dive away from his pursuer. A Type 97 could never outrun a P-40 in a dive, and Rector was able to pour fire from his guns into the Japanese plane. The pilot was desperately trying to get out, yet the slipstream caused by the dive forced him back into the cockpit. Eventually he got out, but at 300 feet. Just as his parachute opened he hit the ground. Other pilots making claims that day were Percy Bartelt, Gil Bright and Johnny Petach. As well as Christman's loss, Bartling's P-40 was so badly damaged that he had to crash-land and Bob Neale had fought so hard that the engine of his plane was burned out. Bartelt's engine had also been giving him trouble, and he had dropped out of the fight early.

On 24 January Japanese air activity was limited to a small raid. Neale and Tex Hill made the intercept. Neale reported, 'They were seven lone, single-engined bombers sneaking in to bomb Mingaladon. About the same time Tex Hill and I dove on them, we saw two . . . Brewster Buffaloes . . . hit them from above. One RAF pilot blew up a bomber in the middle . . . and the rest

BELOW: In March 1942 the AVG received some P-40Es. They had a better performance than the P-40Bs that made up the bulk of their aircraft.

ABOVE: Flying Tiger ace Dick Rossi in a one-piece flying suit.

briefly, and described Hoffman's plane as looking like 'a fish writhing in agony out of water.' Boyington's own attempt to try and turn with a Japanese fighter illustrated just why Chennault had vehemently opposed using such a tactic:

'. . . the entire formation I had been sitting in a second before had disappeared completely. . . . So I pulled off and down to one side to get out from underneath the diving Japs. And what a relief to have free air above me for a change.

'Soon I spotted a pair of Japs off to the side of me, so I added throttle and started to close in behind them. One of these two pulled almost straight up, going into a loop above my P-40 about the same instant I started my tracers toward the other. I knew that I had to break off firing and commence turning, or the Jap who was then above my P-40 would have me bore-sighted.

'Recollection of how I had been able to out turn the best of the United States fleet's pilots in peacetime practices probably gave me self-assurance. . . . I discovered that even hauling back on my stick and pulling with all my might . . . gave me no advantage whatsoever. As a matter of fact, I was sufficiently blacked out not to be able to see whether my bursts had gotten the I-97. . . . All the time I was pulling this terrific g-load, tracers were getting closer to my plane. . . . "Frig this racket" I thought, and dove away.

'In trying once again I gave myself a much better break, making a faster pass from a thousand feet above. As I approached this Nip fighter, he also permitted me to get close enough to where my tracers were sailing about him. Then I witnessed this plane perform one of the most delightful split-Ss I had ever seen, and then I discovered that I was turning again with some of his playmates.

'"To hell with this routine!" I thought, and dove out.'

The Japanese mounted one more big raid on Rangoon in January, three days after Hoffman was killed. In this confused melee the AVG accounted for 17 of the enemy, without loss to themselves.

The Panda Bears and the Adam and Eves were also flying support missions for the Allied troops battling the advancing Japanese around Moulmein and along the Salween River. On one strafing mission, Newkirk, Mickelson, Ed Rector, Bob Prescott, John Croft and Dick Rossi found a Japanese mechanized column advancing through the jungle. They were led by a group of elephants trampling down small trees and undergrowth to provide a smoother path for the light tanks and

started to run. We just knocked them off like moving targets in a shooting gallery.' Two days later Japanese fighters were back. A fighter sweep was intercepted by the Panda Bears and the Adam and Eves, who got up in two sections. Bob Prescott was flying wingman to Louis Hoffman, who had earned the nickname 'Cokey' for his constant quest for supplies of Coca-Cola, then hard to find in the Far East:

'We were climbing at maximum to join the first flight. I saw a bunch of single-engined planes circling high above us. I thought they were our first flight waiting for us. So did the rest of our flight. Suddenly the planes above us were peeling off and diving on us. They hit us while were we still in our 110mph climb. Five of them came down on Cokey and me.

'I looked back and saw one Jap closing the range on me. I jammed the stick forward until it almost touched the instrument panel. I saw the airspeed indicator showed 450mph, and I swore because it wasn't fast enough. I kept shoving forward on the stick, and the indicator hit 515. I felt better then but shuddered when I thought of it later. Anything over 450 was supposed to rip the wings off, but that old P-40 really held together. I never did see what happened to Coke.'

Hoffman had been a victim of the diving attack. Gregory Boyington had seen it

armored cars. The P-40s made their strafing runs, concentrating at first on the elephants. The wounded elephants became enraged and stampeded, kicking over the small, two-man Japanese tankettes.

On 30 January the AVG suffered another casualty when Tommy Cole was shot down after flying a strafing mission over an airfield at Meshod and on Japanese rear-echelon positions in Burma around Kawkareik. By the end of January the Panda Bears had only patched up P-40s left to them. In fact, only six of their original 18 planes were able to fly at all. In the light of this, Chennault ordered the 2nd Pursuit Squadron back to Kunming, and reinforced the eight Adam and Eves at Mingaladon with the rest of their squadron. The air battle for Rangoon was moving into its final stages.

When the Adam and Eves took over in Rangoon the battle for Burma was in full swing. Moulmein had fallen the day before, and the Japanese were pressing against the Allied defensive line along the Salween River. It was a battle that slowly and steadily drew the AVG into its combats and it was also one that had a substantial impact on the ability of the Adam and Eves to carry out their task of defending Burma's seaport.

As the Japanese were to advance farther and farther into Burma, so they occupied the sites that were used to report the approach of Japanese aircraft. The AVG had already had trouble with Rangoon's air raid alerts. In the early days, often the first warn-ing they had of the incoming formations was the sight of RAF fighters taking off in a cloud of dust and heading west. Then the pilots of the AVG knew to get their P-40s airborne as quickly as possible. Things had improved after a while, once the British became aware that their 'Chinese' allies needed some advance information. The Japanese victories to the southeast of Rangoon, however, began to make holes in the network of forward stations, holes that were irreparable.

The Japanese air forces continued their struggle to secure air superiority. The first encounter the Adam and Eves had with their opponents occurred on 3 February. The Japanese came over and were driven off, then came over again the next day. The Adam and Eves' squadron leader, Bob Sandell, brought down five enemy fighters over the two days.

On the 4th Sandell had to retire from the fighting when his engine's cooling system was damaged. He came in to land at Mingaladon, and as he taxied along the runway a Japanese plane, its pilot mortally wounded, swooped in low over Mingaladon on a *kamikaze* strafing run. As the aircraft was losing altitude fast, it clipped the tail of Sandell's P-40 before crashing at the runway's end. The whole tail section of Sandell's plane came off, while the radial engine of the Japanese fighter went bouncing across the field to land right next to a totally unsuspecting Sandell. Sandell's crew had

FAR LEFT: John Donovan, a pilot of the Hell's Angels.

LEFT: Dick Rossi again, this time with a beard and leather jacket.

mended the damaged aircraft within two days, and the squadron leader decided to take it up in a test flight. While performing a roll the tail section of the plane came away, and the P-40 plummeted to the earth. Sandell was killed in the crash, being unable to do anything to save himself. Bob Neale was appointed to command of the Adam and Eves in Sandell's place.

Neale took over at a hectic time. The Adam and Eves were constantly in action. A typical day might see them strafe Moulmein in the morning, escort three bomber missions during the day, while going through anything between two to five alerts of bomber or fighter attacks. The day after Neale took command, Gregory Boyington got his first kill, in an incident that shows how pilots very rarely see the plane that gets them:

'We had taken off twice, during the same alert, and couldn't make contact with any bandits the first time, although reports were coming in from RAF radar control. A hazy day made a will o' the wisp game out of it. Here they are. No, they aren't. Finally, after about two hours of this, I saw one lone Jap fighter, almost across the bay heading into the Sittang River. Apparently he was heading for Moulmein, out of fuel.

'It was simple to ease up behind this I-97, and I had all the time in the world to set my sights for a no-deflection shot. He never saw me, at least not before I fired. Fear that I had missed him was soon over. The I-97 slowly half-rolled and plowed out of sight under the water.'

Two days after Neale assumed command, the Salween River line gave way, and the Japanese were that much closer to Rangoon. The position of the British Imperial forces defending Rangoon deteriorated further with their defeat in a savage series of battles in front of the Bilin River. On 15 February, the same day as the capitulation of the British defenders of Singapore, the British withdrew behind the Bilin. Chennault was worried by the inability of Burma's defenders to slow down the Japanese. When the Bilin line was abandoned on the 19th, and the last obstacle to the Japanese attackers was the Sittang, he ordered the original eight Adam and Eves who had arrived in Rangoon in the middle of January to return to Kunming. Neale was now down to eight pilots, and the engines of the P-40s at his disposal were worn out by the constant flying. Chennault sent him eight fresh aircraft to replace the worn planes, just in time to counter the next series of Japanese attacks.

The first daylight raid attempted in several weeks was made on 25 February, just two days after the British had suffered a disastrous defeat along the Sittang. The Japanese scented a victory and were stepping up the pressure on Rangoon in order to clinch it. Nine of the AVG and six RAF Hurricanes intercepted the raid. The Adam and Eves claimed 13 victims, with Neale and

RIGHT: Chaplain Paul Frillman.

FAR RIGHT: Bob Locke, with friend.

'Black Mac' McGarry being the high scorers, with four apiece. The raid was the first of the final series of attacks on Rangoon. Charlie Bond witnessed the heavy toll the Adam and Eves made the Japanese pay for their fights over the Burmese capital on the first two days:

'The big show started on 25 February. We took off on a false alarm, and Bob Neale decided we might as well strafe Moulmein, which we had planned for later in the day. . . . Coming in low we saw three Japs getting off the runway on a field south of Moulmein. Neale, Bob Little and I dived. Two Japs crashed in flames, and the third was hit. We went on to hit Moulmein field like a ton of bricks.

'We hadn't seen the Jap fighter patrol at 18,000 feet, but they saw us. We had our hands full for a while. . . . Fights broke out all over the sky. We added nine planes to those wrecked at Moulmein.

'Then two fighters got on Neale's tail, and he went tearing out across the Gulf of Martaban at about 50 feet with slugs following him fast. Somehow he shook them off and got home all right.

'In the afternoon the Japanese came over Rangoon with fighters. I've never seen so many fighters in the air. . . . They swarmed all over the sky like flies buzzing around a dead dog. We pitched into them and the slaughter was terrific. The fighters were blowing up all over the sky like bursts of antiaircraft shells. Just a puff of smoke, a ball of flame, and they were gone. We knocked out 13 confirmed. . . .

'Bright and early on the 26th we had an alarm and every plane left the deck. Radio communications weren't so good and we had trouble finding the Japs. . . . [Neale's] flight was ripping into them, but mine still couldn't locate them.

'In the afternoon we sighted 12 bombers and 30 fighters, and we pitched in . . . it was a picnic. Something to shoot at everywhere we looked. Only one bomber went down but we got 18 fighters.'

Neale's hair-raising chase over the Gulf of Martaban, with fighters on his tail, was later recalled by the squadron leader:

'I was plenty scared. Bullets were going through my tail. They made a funny smell of scorched metal I could smell in the cockpit. One broke an oil line. Another hit the instrument panel. I was only at 50 feet when they hit me, so I couldn't dive away. I just sat there and took it, weaving to throw off their aim and jamming the throttle until I thought it would break off. After about 40 miles I began to pull out of range . . . I found out for sure that the P-40 was faster than the

Type 97, but it wasn't fun.'

On 27 February, the British commander in Burma ordered his troops in Rangoon to commence a demolition program before withdrawing from the city. Neale was determined to stick it out as long as he could, and received a message from Chennault to conserve his pilots and planes, but fly out of

ABOVE: The ground crew team that kept the planes of 3rd Pursuit Squadron in the air.

Rangoon 'on last bottle of oxygen.' Neale also hoped to stay long enough for a pilot, Ed Liebolt, who had gone missing on a patrol southwest of Rangoon, to get back. However, Rangoon's radar set was withdrawn on the 27th, leaving the AVG to defend their base with no form of early warning. The Japanese squadrons were also in this predicament, and the AVG's constant strafing that left smoking wreckage sitting on the runways was a reminder to Neale of what could happen to his planes.

In the light of this, Neale ordered the Adam and Eves to abandon Rangoon. The bulk of the pilots flew to Magwe early on 28 February. Neale hung around, with his aircraft specially prepared to take a passenger in case Liebolt should turn up. The radio equipment had been removed, leaving a space behind the cockpit that would provide uncomfortable accommodation for a man. When the time came to go, there was no sign of Liebolt, so Neale shoved a couple of cases of whiskey into the space and took off for Magwe.

Chennault could draw several important lessons from the fighting over Rangoon, lessons that could influence his tactical and strategic choices later in the war. The most important was the vindication of his faith in the ability of pursuit aviation to defend a chosen position, provided it had sufficient warning to get into the air and intercept the attackers. Rangoon's warning system was not as efficient as Chennault would have liked, yet it proved good enough to deny the Japanese in their attempts to gain air superiority over the Burmese capital for three months. The reason for the AVG's ultimate defeat illustrates the truth of the saying, 'The best air superiority weapon is a tank on the runway.'

However, though the AVG were never defeated in the air, one has to conclude that it was only a matter of time before they would have been. The Japanese air forces available considerably outnumbered those of the Allies, and the wear and tear on the P-40s flown by the AVG was considerable, even if their losses in combat were small. The dust of Mingaladon was so bad that each day ground crews had to take apart the

BELOW: The status board of the 3rd Pursuit Squadron. Charlie Older, Parker Dupouy and Fred Hodges are on patrol.

carburetors and clean them out. To help with field maintenance, ground crews assembled salvage teams that searched the countryside around Rangoon to find wrecks. These would be stripped of anything that might help keep a P-40 flying. Metal skin from other aircraft could be used to patch bullet holes, and the rubber tires of another plane were invaluable, for the AVG had a very limited supply, and the constant taking off and landing wore out those they did have very quickly.

Once the P-40s were in need of a complete overhaul, it was necessary to pull the aircraft back to the CAMCO factory at Loiwing, where the work could be done. The stress on fighter pilots constantly flying missions could only be fixed by taking them out of the front line and giving them some time off. Chennault was forced to adopt his policy of rotating his squadrons in and out of Rangoon in order to spare the material he had least reserves of: trained fighter pilots. All these operations were taxed to their limits, and a failure of one would have fatally compromised the pilots' efforts.

The AVG was also assisted in its defense by the errors of the Japanese. At first they relied on the prewar principle that 'the bomber will get through.' Unescorted formations proved sitting ducks for the more nimble P-40s. It was a lesson that had to be learned in turn by each air force during the war. The Japanese adopted a two-fold approach to rectifying deficiencies in its ability to protect bombers. Like the Germans and Americans it began sending escorted formations over during the day; like the British, the Japanese used area bombing at night, albeit on a much smaller scale. Yet these solutions, just as in Europe, had their own shortcomings. Night bombing on such a small scale was ineffectual in destroying what became a pinpoint target in the darkness. Escort missions raised all the problems of choosing how to escort the bombers, and how many fighters to send over. Japanese doctrine was to provide one fighter for every three bombers, and they followed doctrine as best they could. This scale was inadequate for the job in hand, and eventually they pretty much reversed the ratio.

What they never really overcame was how to deploy the fighters they had effectively. These highly maneuverable planes were at first forced to carry out escort missions that tied them closely to cumbersome bomber formations, negating their advantage over the less maneuverable P-40s. Escorting fighters usually hand the initiative over to their attackers, yet Japanese fighters, whether Type 96s, Type 97s, or Type 0s, were designed to be used aggressively.

When the bomber raids were supplanted by fighter sweeps, this freed the Japanese pilots to take aggressive action in finding and attacking AVG pilots in the air. These were no more successful than the bomber attacks were at clearing the skies of Allied opposition. Sweeps, in addition, are a very costly method of waging air warfare. The RAF's attempts at fighter sweeps over northwestern France in 1942 produced an unfavorable balance of losses, and the same thing happened to the Japanese over Rangoon. Pilots like fighter sweeps, but they are not efficient.

Furthermore, Japanese fighter tactics were not well adapted to their machines. Just like the AVG, Japanese pilots were trained to attack the target in a series of hit-and-run passes. The only difference was their aircraft's ability to perform a scissors – a sharp reversal of direction in a turn in order to get on an opponent's tail – well, and their willingness, compared to AVG pilots, to try it. However, the scissors maneuver only really works if the opponent tries to follow suit, and the AVG pilots had been carefully instructed not to. The Japanese, ironically, seem to have played into Chennault's hands by their reluctance to start an air combat off as a turning, or angles, fight. Both sides were fighting with similar tactics, tactics that suited the P-40 a lot better than they did any of the Japanese fighters.

Finally, the Japanese consistently gave a respite to the AVG, just at the point when the balance of air fighting might have tipped in their favor. After only two days of raids on 23 and 25 December Chennault reckoned the Hell's Angels had had enough. Yet the Japanese did not attack again until January. The first week in January saw heavy fighting, but again the Japanese paused, giving Chennault a chance to move in replacement pilots from the Adam and Eves. Toward the end of the month there was another flurry of action, followed by another pause, and the Panda Bears were replaced by the rest of the Adam and Eves. Just as Japanese fighter pilots played to AVG strengths, so did their operational planners.

Chennault and his pilots were fortunate. Yet good fortune without talent is worthless, just as talent without good fortune is wasted. In the end the Japanese won the air battle of Rangoon, but it was a Pyrrhic victory, and one that owed little to any triumphs of their pilots. The AVG demonstrated that its pilots were better trained, and better shots.

THE war that the AVG, now popularly known as the Flying Tigers in the world's press, fought after the fall of Rangoon had a very different character to the battles for Burma's capital. Whereas the first three months of fighting had been a point defense campaign, the rest of their combat record in Burma was shaped by demands created by the fighting on the ground. The British and Imperial Army in Burma had begun 'the longest retreat in its history' and what it sought from its air support was top cover over its columns of troops, and strafing runs against Japanese troop movements.

Fighter pilots don't like either of these kinds of missions. Covering a column of men or vehicles is dull work in which the pilots may lose concentration as they try to keep pace with a much more slowly moving earthbound force. Strafing is dangerous. A

and Eves; or all but one, Bob Neale choosing to stay behind for more action. Neale in fact refused to return to Kunming for rest until special orders from Chennault arrived on 13 March. Neale had been one of the first contingent of Adam and Eves to arrive at Mingaladon back in January. His 60 days of combat duty was the longest stretch that any of the Flying Tigers would complete.

The Hell's Angels, which after all were part of the Chinese Air Force, now had Chinese troops to fly support missions for. Chiang Kai-shek had released three armies to help the British defend Burma and one division concentrated around Toungoo in early March. One regular mission, usually flown by Fred Hodges, was to carry intelligence reports based on the information gathered by the reconnaissance flights flown by the Flying Tigers to Chinese head-

CHAPTER 5

THE LONG RETREAT

pilot has to fly in a straight line very fast at a low altitude. There is little room for a mistake – a false move and plane and pilot are scattered over the ground. The predictable flight path and need for attentiveness to accurate shooting make a strafing aircraft vulnerable to attack from above. A strafing pilot also has to worry about fire from the smallarms of the target of his attack, and the possibility that a lucky shot will disable his aircraft.

The Adam and Eves who pulled out of Rangoon flew on to Magwe, an RAF base halfway up the River Irrawaddy from the Burmese capital. Their new base was farther away from the ones used by the Japanese squadrons and the range of the Flying Tigers' P-40s was stretched to the utmost for their strafing raids. Toward the end of the first week of March, Parker Dupouy and 11 pilots from the Hell's Angels arrived at Magwe to relieve the tired Adam

quarters at Lashio and Toungoo. The AVG had not been trained for ground-support operations, but as the Flying Tigers flew more strafing missions, they became more experienced in their techniques. Parker Dupouy flew a mission with Cliff Groh, Moose Moss and Ken Jernstedt along the Sittang River that revealed a particular weakness in the Flying Tigers' approach:

'We found the Japs ferrying part of an armored division across the river in barges. We hit the river barges first, sinking two loaded with tanks. The Japs dived off the rest of the barges as we came over them. We hit the compound [of trucks and armored cars], setting a dozen trucks and scout cars on fire, and took one last swipe at some railroad cars sitting on the siding near the wrecked railroad bridge [destroyed on a mission the day before]. They must have been full of something, because they sure burned.

ABOVE: Three Japanese Type 89 medium tanks cross a bridge over a Burmese stream. A wrecked British ambulance lies in the muddy waters.

LEFT: A Japanese infantry column crosses a footbridge beside a demolished railroad bridge to the south of Moulmein in Burma. Once Rangoon had fallen, Burma was indefensible. All the Allied forces could do was delay the Japanese advance by demolitions, rearguard stands and harassment from the air.

RIGHT: Ground crewman 'Twisty' Bent. While the pilots could fly out of a threatened airfield to one in a less vulnerable position, the mechanics and other service personnel had to make long and dangerous journeys along the Burmese roads.

BELOW: A hangar at Toungoo, the AVG's first home, after a surprise Japanese bombing raid.

'Coming back, we were scooting along under the overcast with not much visibility when I heard Moose Moss yell over the radio, ''Bandits above!'' There were six Nakajima Type 97 fighters in the hazy clouds above, getting ready to dive on our tails. Moss shot one down before we knew they were there and the rest disappeared. That was the last time we made a strafe without somebody above as top cover to protect our tails.'

The Japanese, however, had things pretty much their own way in the air war during March and April. The AVG and RAF squadrons present at Magwe did their best to support the troops on the ground, but they were heavily outnumbered and could not be everywhere they were needed. Yet even such tactical successes as the raid on Moulmein by two of the Flying Tigers on 18 March could not transform the strategic situation. The night before Bill Reed and Ken Jernstedt found themselves at Toungoo, and chose to do a reconnaissance over Moulmein airfield to see just what the Japanese might have up their sleeves. They arrived to find the place packed with fighters and bombers, so they made several strafing runs just at dawn, about 0755 hours. The attack netted the single highest total of aircraft destroyed on a mission in the whole of the Flying Tigers' career.

Such a strike could only move the Japanese to action and they hit back hard. On 20 March, while Dupouy was patrolling

up the Irrawaddy, he heard a report on his radio that Magwe was under attack. He turned round and 10 minutes from the field spotted 27 bombers coming back. The six Flying Tigers attacked and scored some successes. Dupouy, teamed with Jernstedt, helped account for three bombers, then tangled with eight Type 0s and got one of those. He turned to attack another bomber flight, making its run over Magwe, when he

ABOVE: Medals, certificates, insignia and a blood chit belonging to an AVG pilot.

LEFT: Ground crewman Ed Forbes slapped this Flying Tiger decal on his suitcase. It originally had been on the fuselage of a P-40.

Flying Tigers

The origin of the AVG's nickname the 'Flying Tigers' is something of a mystery. The choice of the animal was almost certainly related to the Chinese Republic's adoption of the tiger as its national animal, supplanting the dragon of bygone imperial days. The shark's teeth painted along the noses of the P-40s gave rise to the story that the tiger shark was regarded as especially unlucky by Japanese fishermen. Flying Tigers rolls off the tongue rather more easily than Flying Tiger Sharks, and ties in with patriotic Chinese symbolism.

Another version holds that Chinese newspapers called the AVG the *Fei Hu*, or Flying Tigers, and the rest of the world's press simply adopted it to serve as a considerably more colorful handle than American Volunteer Group. Naturally, the AVG wound up with a playful tiger cub to serve as a mascot.

The Walt Disney studio were informed by Chennault of the nickname and designed a badge to go with it. A 'V' (for victory) lying on its side had a winged tiger racing out of it. A first issue of the badges was made at a dinner held at the University of Kunming in February 1942. Some 300 Chinese political dignitaries assembled to honor pilots of the Hell's Angels and Panda Bears. Madame Chiang Kai-shek passed out the badges.

LEFT: An AVG pin and the Order of the National Army, Navy and Air Force.

ABOVE LEFT: A medal awarded to AVG pilots.

ABOVE: The Chinese cap insignia.

had to break off action after running out of ammunition. Two Type 0s attacked as he was landing, wounding him and destroying his P-40.

Jernstedt, who also had to land, was strafed as he touched down and his face was badly cut by broken glass from his windshield. The four others, Fritz Wolf, Bob Prescott, Bill Reed and Moose Moss, attacked some Type 97s whose pilots knew just how to fly against P-40s. They timed turns to perfection as the Flying Tigers came diving in to make their hit-and-run attacks, and the P-40s eventually ran out of gas and had to land. The field at Magwe was devastated by the raid, which had involved some 90 enemy aircraft. RAF bombers were burning wrecks and explosions continued for an hour after the last Japanese bomb had been dropped. The only true success was the shooting down of a Japanese fighter by three AVG ground crew firing pistols and sub-machine guns – Joseph Sweeney, Manning Wakefield and Keith Christensen.

The next day the Japanese were back. The lone RAF radar set, which was in a position only to be able to detect attacks from the south, had been withdrawn and the airfield had no warning whatsoever. Mechanics were working on aircraft parked out in the open when the rumble of twin-engined bombers' engines gave the first alert of the strike. The P-40 pilots had to eat dirt as they hid in slit trenches to avoid the bombs. One, Frank Swartz, was fatally wounded by an explosion and died a month later at a hospital in Poona, India. Crew chief John Fauth was also fatally wounded, dying the same day. All but two of the P-40s were damaged, while the RAF was wiped out. Magwe was abandoned. It marked the lowest point in the AVG's history.

Even an attempt to strike back at the Japanese got mixed results. Ten P-40s flew out of Loi-wing and stopped to refuel at RAF landing strips in Burma, four at He-ho and six at Nam Sang. The He-ho contingent was led by Jack Newkirk and his mission was to hit Lampun airfield. When they got there, they found no Japanese aircraft, so had to turn round and go home disappointed. On their way back they spotted a mechanized column. Newkirk decided to strafe it and get some value out of the mission, but on the first pass his plane must have been hit by ground fire; it dived into the ground and exploded, killing the ace pilot. Neale's flight of six included Greg Boyington:

'All we had for bearing on take off from the rolling dirt strip [Nam Sang] were a couple of trucks parked on the field with their headlights on dim. Everybody got off

. . . no running lights. Merely the reddish glare from our own exhaust stacks to fly formation on.

'What was passing by in the jungle below us, or how close we came to any mountains, was in my imagination only. Finally, light started to appear in the sky above us, and then I could begin to see dim outlines below me.

'At about this same time our lead planes turned sharp left like they were going to run into a mountain. They started to dive. I wheeled my plane and dove after them, although I couldn't make out any target as yet. Even before I saw the field I saw tracers from the guns of my mates preceding me. Then the field seemed to take shape in the semi-darkness. I sighted in on the same place where the previous tracers had gone, some of these tracers were visible ricocheting as if being fired from the opposite direction.

'The first pass got three transports ablaze, which, owing to their size, were the easiest to pick out that time of the morning. In turn the burning transports helped to light up our target area as we wheeled around for a pass in the opposite direction. I don't see how any of us knew which one was which.

BELOW: Armorer Chuck Baisden checks out a machine gun on an antiaircraft mounting. When an AVG airfield was under attack, the ground crew manned the antiaircraft weapons.

'The second pass was made under much better visibility, even in those few seconds it took to turn around. It was evident our attack had come as a complete surprise, for I strafed down a line of planes that were parked as I remembered before the war at old Squadron II at the navy training center in Pensacola, Florida.

'I could see blurred forms jumping off wings, out of cockpits, and scurrying all over the field like ants. I made two more passes, witnessing fires all over the Chiengmai airfield.

'By the time we made the last couple of passes the air was so full of black puffs of antiaircraft fire it was difficult to determine whether the Japs had launched any aircraft, or even to see our other P-40s.

'Radio silence was broken finally when someone yelled: ''Let's get the Hell out of here.'''

The black puffs did manage to claim one victim, Black Mac McGarry. Damage forced him to bail out. He was listed during the war as missing in action, but had been captured and was interned by the Thai government. The loss of Newkirk, a popular character, hit the Flying Tigers hard. They were also unhappy about morale-boosting missions that Chiang Kai-shek required them to fly over Chinese troop positions. On these they flew at a height of about 1000 feet in a tight, three-plane formation that was vulnerable to being bounced by enemy fighters. Ground fire was sometimes heavy, and they were supposed to fly straight and level so Chinese infantrymen could get a good look at the insignia on the planes. On one occasion in April, three P-40s appeared over Pyinmana to boost the morale of some Chinese under heavy pressure from the advancing Japanese. They were surprised

to be met by heavy antiaircraft fire. The pilots blamed the Chinese, until they found out that Pyinmana had fallen to the Japanese the day before.

Dissatisfaction and frustration were not helped by frequent Japanese raids and reconnaissances over Loi-wing, where the AVG now had its main operational base. On 20 April Chennault ordered some of the pilots to fly an escort mission for RAF bombers. The command touched off a near mutiny. A petition against unpopular missions was organized and handed to Tex Hill, squadron leader at Loi-wing. Hill eventually got some volunteers to fly with him and perform the escort mission, but there were recriminations over the incident. A number of pilots resigned, and were given dishonorable discharges. The morale-boosting missions were halted.

The only tonic that would help the Flying Tigers would be a successful combat. Japanese troops were moving up the Salween River valley and Loi-wing was bombed on 25 April. Bombing Loi-wing cost the Japanese six fighters, including one flown by an exceptionally experienced pilot.

LEFT: Another of the 3rd Pursuit Squadron's aces, 'Catfish' Raines.

BELOW: Japanese planes leave oil storage tanks in flames. The air war during March and April in Burma was one of ground-attack raids on airfields, columns of troops and valuable targets such as these oil tanks.

ABOVE: AVG pilot Bob Prescott makes use of local transport.

The First Red River Rats

On 12 May seven Flying Tigers began a long flight to Hanoi in their P-40s. The stunt was the idea of a daring member of the group, Tom Jones, and the men who carried it out were all volunteers. The seven — Jones, Tex Hill, Lewis Bishop, Frank Schiel, Link Laughlin, Jim Howard and Johnny Donovan — first flew to Mengtsz, tangling with a monsoon thunderstorm over Yunnan. There they took on ammunition and bombs, as well as refueling. Howard's P-40 developed engine trouble and he had to fly back to Kunming.

The six remaining flew on to reach the Hanoi airfield just before dusk. To guide them en route they followed the Red River down from the mountains. They attacked out of the sun at twilight. The first sweep blasted a few aircraft. Donovan's plane was hit by antiaircraft fire, crashed and burned. A transport plane took several passes to destroy.

Twelve Type 97s took to the air and chased the departing P-40s. One caught Schiel as he was climbing away, the instant when the P-40 was most vulnerable, but once he had leveled out he easily outran his pursuer.

A second raid was led by Lewis Bishop on 17 May. Hanoi aerodrome was again shot up but Bishop, in an unguarded moment, announced to his comrades over the radio that they should hit Lao Ky airfield. The antiaircraft guns were waiting for them, and Bishop was shot down and interned by the Vichy French authorities.

It took 20 minutes to shoot him down. On the 29th, the emperor's birthday, Chennault once again successfully predicted a Japanese attack, this one on Lashio and Loiwing. Sixteen P-40s were airborne as two large formations of fighter and bombers approached. Although the runway was cratered, the Flying Tigers accounted for 22 Japanese planes, mostly fighters, in a fierce aerial engagement. They suffered no loss.

Defeat in the field, this time of the Chinese armies, again forced the AVG to withdraw. Lashio was occupied by the Japanese on 29 April, and Loi-wing was evacuated the next day. Most of the group was based at Kunming, but Neale and four other pilots were stationed at the city of Paoshan, about 250 miles to the west. The Japanese advance to the Chinese border with Burma had necessitated abandoning

several warning net sites, and the now-imperfect system failed on 4 May, when a heavy Japanese raid savaged Paoshan. Only two P-40s got airborne, while another pilot, Ben Foshee, was killed by a bomb. Type 0s hanging around the airfield nearly accounted for Charlie Bond, who didn't notice them when he returned. He was badly burned when his plane was shot up and was lucky to survive bailing out at a mere 1000 feet. The Japanese attempted to repeat their feat the next day but Chennault, with the help of very complete intelligence as to the bombers' time of departure, set up a perfect interception. Eight planes of the first wave were shot down, while the second wave did not dare to press its attack, turning tail and running.

The greatest victory the Flying Tigers scored was yet to come. The Japanese in

Burma were now in a position to take Kunming in China by the back door. There was little organized Chinese resistance between Loi-wing and Kunming and the main obstacle to a Japanese advance was the destroyed road bridge across the deep Salween gorge. The Japanese Army was moving pontoons up from Rangoon, however, to construct a replacement and Chennault was concerned that they might be about to push on to Kunming. He now had at his disposal some P-40Es, equipped with six .50 caliber machine guns and bomb racks. These had flown all the way from West Africa to Kunming, quite a remarkable ferrying operation. He ordered four of them to be bombed up for a ground-attack mission.

All Japanese troops and supplies had to be moved along a twisting road that clung to one side of the Salween gorge. The P-40Es, operating with four P-40Bs flying top cover, struck just as engineers were getting to work on the pontoon bridge. Bombs were carefully aimed to strike the side of the gorge, causing landslides and blocking the road. They then blasted the pontoons and engineering vehicles with fragmentation bombs and machine-gunned the vehicles now strewn along the road.

This was just the first raid of a three-day operation that caused the Japanese to abandon further advances up the Salween during 1942. The monsoon was closing in, and would make it extremely difficult to

ABOVE: A P-40E warms up its engine before taking off on a mission.

ABOVE RIGHT: A P-40E taxis past Chinese workers.

RIGHT: Chennault's pilots scramble for their aircraft at an airfield in China.

supply any campaign in northern Burma. The strafing marked the last Flying Tiger operation in the area. Future missions would be made in China, where the pilots had expected to fight when they originally signed contracts.

The history of the AVG was coming to a close. Since the end of December the US Army Air Force had been pressing for the induction of the group into its ranks, despite the fact that most of its pilots came from the navy. Chennault agreed to return to his old service and was given the rank of brigadier general. He would also be in charge of aerial operations in China, but his men, however, proved unwilling to join him. Most wanted to go home, if only for just 30 days, which they were entitled to. They were tired and homesick. Some just didn't want to join the air force, preferring to return to their original branch of the services. Chennault only managed to get five pilots and 25 ground crew to

PREVIOUS PAGES: A P-40 banked in a turn.

BELOW: Mechanics of the Fourteenth Air Force go over P-40s before a mission. The Fourteenth Air Force, commanded by Chennault adopted the AVG's shark's teeth for their own planes.

sign up. It was heartbreaking.

The AVG was scheduled to cease its existence on 4 July 1942. The month of June saw it strike a few last blows against the Japanese, and suffer a few casualties. Bob Little was killed bombing a Japanese gun position on 22 May, while John Donovan was killed over Hanoi on 12 May. Lewis Bishop was captured when he was shot down over Lao Ky airfield in Indochina on 17 May. During a raid on the Chinese city of Kweilin on 13 June five Japanese fighters were added to the Flying Tigers' claims. Some bombers, B-25s, arrived from India in late June, and were used in several raids on Hankow during the last week of the AVG's existence. Bob Neale, now the AVG's top ace, and Charlie Bond shot down a fighter together on 4 July in the last Flying Tiger combat.

At midnight on 4 July 1942, the Flying Tigers were disbanded.

IN less than a year of combat the AVG claimed to have shot down 299 Japanese aircraft. It can be demonstrated by examination of claims and actual losses that fighter pilots invariably exaggerate the exact number of their kills, but the effect of aerial operations is not determined by some profit and loss balance sheet. What counts is the effect of your own aerial actions on enemy air operations and plans, and the AVG's effectiveness was considerable. The Flying Tigers had prevented the Japanese from establishing air supremacy over southern Burma, and they reduced the Japanese ability to interfere with the withdrawal of Allied troops from central and northern Burma. They blocked the Japanese advance up the Salween gorge and also reduced the number and frequency of Japanese bombing raids on Nationalist Chinese cities. All

CHAPTER 6

ASSESSMENT

this was accomplished in less than one year's existence by some 60 pilots and a couple of hundred ground crew.

For the five who stayed on, Tex Hill, Gil Bright, Ed Rector, Frank Schiel and Charlie Sawyer, there was the task of helping Chennault establish the China Air Task Force. This originally consisted of four fighter squadrons and a bomber squadron, and interfered substantially with Japanese supply lines in southern China. They flew better equipment, later model P-40s, and the bombers gave them a punch the AVG lacked until its last week of existence.

The Task Force lasted for eight months. In April 1943 Roosevelt and the Joint Chiefs of Staff held a summit in Washington to hammer out a strategy for China. General Joseph Stilwell, the commander of the American forces in the China-Burma-India theater, and chief of staff of Chiang Kai-shek's armies attended, as did Major General Claire Chennault, promoted in

ABOVE: P-40s of the Fourteenth Air Force.

LEFT: A ground crewman paints the China Air Task Force symbol on to a plane.

ABOVE RIGHT: Chinese laborers flatten a runway with a roller. China's vast reservoir of manpower was used to perform many tasks that were mechanized on other fronts.

RIGHT: A line-up of Task Force P-40s.

PREVIOUS PAGES: The new insignia for the Flying Tigers. Uncle Sam's hat indicates a change in ownership.

ABOVE: A P-40 painted in the Flying Tiger color scheme on a runway.

LEFT: Chennault with the staff of his new air command in China in 1942. The rickety administration of AVG days had now given way to the smooth-running corporate-style typical of the US armed forces.

RIGHT: As well as staff, equipment came in better quantities than before. Damaged parts not longer had to be repaired overnight. These damaged propellers are awaiting repair.

BELOW: Ben Thompson, one of Chennault's pilots in the Fourteenth Air Force, pictured in 1944.

March and given command of the newly-formed 14th Air Force in China. Ironically, for a man who had stood firmly against the idea that bombers could win a war single-handed, Chennault was in favor of waging in China a purely aerial campaign. He assured President Roosevelt that air power would be the triumphant instrument of victory, that all Chiang Kai-shek's armies would have to do would be to advance in the wake of aerial attacks, overrunning the positions of a shattered Japanese Army. Chennault had in mind, perhaps, the Flying Tigers' assault on the Japanese in the Salween gorge as the model for this successful campaign. He could, as an example of the power of bombardments, also point to the complete collapse of civil order in Rangoon during February and March 1942, the war's sole vindication of the prewar theorists.

To Stilwell this was stuff and nonsense. The Chinese war would have to be won by armies on the ground. Diverting valuable supply capacity to serve Chennault's flyboys would prevent Chiang Kai-shek's armies from ever attaining the standards of a modern fighting force. Futhermore, the Japanese would simply do to Chennault's bases in China what they had done to the Flying Tigers in Rangoon: capture their airfields with military operations.

In the event, Stilwell was proved correct, and Chennault wrong. The Flying Tigers' achievements were replicated, and the Japanese launched an offensive in 1944 that came close to knocking Chiang Kai-shek out of the war. The effects of the submarine war America was waging against Japan had more to do with halting the Japanese attacks than Chinese victories on the ground or 14th Air Force triumphs in the air.

When a reorganization plan for Chinese and American forces was set out in the spring of 1945, the 14th Air Force's role in the war was marginalized. Chennault owed a lot of his opportunities to the support he received in the staff rooms of Washington

from Roosevelt. But the death of his patron in April left Chennault at the mercy of those who found his unorthodox approach to war and his prickly personality a little too much to bear. He chose to retire and on 1 August left the Army Air Force.

In retirement he continued to work for Chiang Kai-shek, setting up China Air Transport (which later became Civil Air Transport and then Air America). This did sterling work in shipping UN relief supplies to northern China in 1946, but became entangled in the Chinese Civil War and the French war against the Viet Minh in Indochina. Chennault found himself on the losing side in both of these conflicts. His last

ABOVE: New plane, old guise: a P-51 with the shark's teeth painted on the nose. Tex Hill is clambering into the cockpit of a fighter far superior to the one he scored his victories with back in his AVG days.

RIGHT: One of Chiang Kai-shek's men stands guard over a P-40 in its hangar.

years were spent as one of the spokesmen for the China Lobby, the American supporters of Chiang Kai-shek's exiled regime on Taiwan, and as a stern backer of a hawkish stance in the Cold War. When he died in 1958 he was touting an idea: why not set up an international squadron of pilots to help the Laotians and South Vietnamese resist the threat from Hanoi?

His former pilots went on to mixed futures. Greg Boyington and Jim Howard received the Congressional Medal of Honor for heroism in the war. Boyington eventually was accorded the high accolade of a television series based on his exploits flying in the South Pacific with VMF-214, the 'Black Sheep.' Another pilot helped form a cargo-carrying airline known today throughout the world as the Flying Tiger Lines. Some ended up rather less well off. Most retired from their respective services at the war's end, and went on deservingly to enjoy the comforts of civilian life, having certainly led full military careers.

RIGHT: The Flying Tiger Line was begun by some veterans of the Fourteenth Air Force, and has kept the famous name in the public eye.

LEFT: B-25 bombers of the China Air Task Force.

BELOW LEFT: Fourteenth Air Force pilots scrambling before a mission.

BELOW: The P-40N was the last version in a long line of Curtiss fighters. P-40s were never war winners, but they could do most jobs reasonably well.

LEFT: Chennault meets with some of the pilots of his command. Though he reconsidered his strategic ideas in the course of the war, his views on leadership never altered. He remained a pilot's general, always sensitive to his men's needs, and aware that the personal touch counts for a lot. The 'old man' was loyal to his men.

ABOVE: Chennault wears the pilot's wings of the Chinese Air Service on his right breast, and of the US Air Corps on his left. He was to carry his devotion to Chiang Kai-shek's cause with him into retirement.

OVERLEAF: Chennault with Lieutenant General 'Hap' Arnold, commander of the US Army Air Force.

When Roosevelt was pondering the formation of the AVG, back in 1940, he was shown a poem by A E Housman, *Epitaph on an Army of Mercenaries*. It helped him to make up his mind in favor of the scheme. Today, the words of its last verse bring to mind just what the exploits of the Flying Tigers meant to people preoccupied with the fall of Singapore and the loss of the Philippines, who saw Australia and Hawaii threatened, and knew disasters on other fronts and in other places:

Their shoulders held the sky suspended;
They stood, and earth's foundations stay;
What God abandoned, these defended,
And saved the sum of things for pay.

ACKNOWLEDGMENTS

The author and publishers would like to thank Ron Callow for designing this book, Mandy Little for the picture research and Ron Watson for compiling the index. The following agencies and individuals provided photographic material:

Austin Brown/Aviation Picture Library, pages: 2(bottom), 10, 62-63, 66-67, 70(top), 75(top).
Chinese News Agency, pages: 8(top), 9(top).
Hoover Institute, page: 6.
Robert Hunt Library, pages: 4, 8(bottom), 9(bottom), 19(bottom), 26(top), 29(top), 30(bottom), 34, 36(bottom), 37(bottom), 41(bottom), 58(bottom), 60, 68(both), 69(bottom), 73, 74(top), 75(bottom).
Imperial War Museum, London, pages: 27(middle), 38, 61(both), 64-65, 71(top), 74(bottom).
Mainichi Newspapers, page: 24.
Peter Newark's Military Pictures, pages: 2(top), 20.
Larry Pistole, pages: 1, 12(both), 13(both), 14(all three), 15(all three), 16, 17, 18, 19(top), 21, 22(both), 23(all three), 26(bottom), 27(top & bottom), 28, 29(both bottom), 30(top), 31, 32, 33(both), 36(top two), 37(top), 39(both), 40(all three), 41(top), 42, 43, 44(both), 45(both), 46-47, 48, 50, 53(both), 54(both), 55(both), 56, 57, 58(top), 59, 70(bottom), 77(insert), 78.
Warren Thompson, page: 71(bottom).
US Air Force, pages: 72, 76-77.